THE GENIUS OF DESIGN

THE GENIUS OF DESIGN

PENNY SPARKE

First published in 2009 by Quadrille Publishing Limited
Alhambra House
27–31 Charing Cross Road
London WC2H 0LS

wall to wall
A Shedmedia® Company

www.walltowall.co.uk

Editorial director: Jane O'Shea
Project director: Simon Willis
Design: SMITH®: Victoria Forrest, Namkwan Cho
Project editor: Sarah Mitchell
Editor: Simon Davis
Picture researchers: Fiona Fisher, Anne-Marie Hoines,
Claire Limpus, Samantha Rolfe and Melanie Watson
Editorial assistant: Sarah Jones
Production director: Vincent Smith
Production controller: Ruth Deary

For the television series:
Series producer: Tim Kirby
Executive producer: Alex Graham

Cataloguing-in-Publication Data: a catalogue record for this book
is available from the British Library.

ISBN 978 184400 753 0

Printed and bound in Germany

The roundel logo, known as the 'bull's eye' or 'target' was
fully developed for London's Underground by the Arts & Crafts
calligrapher Edward Johnston (1872–1944) in the early years of the
twentieth century. It is wittily re-created **previous pages** by James
Ireland, with a pen and a roll of tape, in response to a commission
by Art on the Underground on the occasion of the 100th anniversary
of the symbol.

The Bugatti Type 57SC 'Atlantic' **following pages**, designed in the
1930s, is one of the twentieth century's most evocative forms. It
demonstrates how, at its best, design can transform a functional
artefact into a sensuous work of art. The car's sleek, integrated
body-shell shows how design can package technology and turn
a machine into a piece of sculpture.

INTRODUCTION

Design is all around us. It's there in the boardroom and on the battlefield; on the factory floor and down the supermarket aisle; in our cars and kitchens; on advertising hoardings and food packaging; on movie sets and in computer avatars. However, design is not just a feature of our surroundings, it is also a process. When we buy a table, arrange flowers in a vase or present a meal we all engage with design and – on one level – become designers ourselves, constantly arranging and re-arranging our surroundings and the objects within them to make our worlds look and work in the way we want. But so caught up are we with the daily routines of our lives that we seldom stop to ask why our environments are as they are: why, that is, things look and perform as they do. This book is an attempt to offer an explanation.

Of course the story of design is set in the context of the other forces that have shaped modern life – economics, politics, technology, culture, society, our psychological make-up, ethics and the world's ecological systems, among them. The way we have designed, and continue to design our world is linked to many facts about ourselves. We have, for example, opted to acquire goods through a system of financial exchange – goods are designed so that people will buy them. Design is a specialised part of the production of goods – we buy things that, for the most part, have been designed and made by others. We like to express our individuality and we jostle with each other for positions on the social ladder, and we want the design of our surroundings to reflect our character and our position. We like to explore the world we live in and to develop and implement new knowledge, and we visualise and make things to help us do this. Design is linked to all these facts and many more. It is, above all else, a reflection of our diverse cultures and a driving force behind their formation.

The stylised stone head of an eagle is, in fact, a gargoyle protruding from one of New York City's most evocative inter-war skyscrapers, the Chrysler Building, which was created as the headquarters of that prestigious automobile company. Designed by William Van Alen the metal-clad building is a masterpiece of Art Deco architecture and its ornamentation, the gargoyles included, is based on features used in the Chrysler automobile.

The story of design here focuses on its modern definition, as a result of the separation of 'designing' from 'making' that occurred in Britain in the second half of the eighteenth century and which, a century and a half later, still has a significant impact all over the world. That is not to say that design didn't exist before that time. Indeed, arguably, it came into being when the first pot was made on the banks of a Mesopotamian river. The stories of hand-making (craft), and of the decorative, or the applied arts, are too long and complex to narrate here, however. Rather, this account focuses on design in the context of the processes and products of industry and their effect on our lives from the middle of the eighteenth century to the present day.

The word 'design', unlike 'art', has a double meaning. Both a verb and a noun, it is not just a feature of our surroundings, it is also the creative process that makes them possible. Uniquely, design bridges the concerns of aesthetics, manufacturing, purchasing and use, in many, sometimes complex, ways. Through its close links with the economic systems of production and consumption, design is much nearer than its cultural neighbours – art, photography, music and literature among them – to the marketplace. It forces culture and commerce to encounter each other in what can often be tense situations; ones, indeed, that have troubled many designers over the years but that have also engendered some of our most lasting objects. Design's recurrent aspiration to become an art form is, however, a sign of its need, at times, to conceal its mass-production and mass-market roots.

Designed spaces, images and objects give us, and our lives, meaning: that is, they both help to form and carry our cultural values. Like fine artists, designers often act as cultural critics. This high cultural role for design is complemented, however, by the important part it plays within the anonymous, everyday world of popular culture.

The Genius of Design outlines the key features of design's journey from the mid-eighteenth century to the present.

The Finnish architect Alvar Aalto's elegant and timeless 'Savoy' glass vase, designed in 1937, produced by Iittala (originally by Karhula), is shown with its original mould; it was created for the Paris World's Fair of that year. Its curvaceous form is said to reflect the contours of Finland's many lakes although another explanation is that it accommodates flowers of different lengths.

Some histories of design have focused on objects (usually iconic ones) and their formal properties, while others have emphasised the importance of named designers. Yet others have seen design as synonymous with the material culture of everyday life and ignored the world of professional design and the numerous creative individuals who have enhanced our modern material world. This account embraces the mundane *and* the special, the amateur *and* the professional, taste *and* style, and high *and* popular culture. Above all it focuses on the human interaction with design as it relates to production, creative practice (both professional and amateur), consumption and use. While the main thrust is broadly chronological, its five chapters are thematically focused. Its main geographical emphasis is Europe and America – the homes of modern design – although a more global context is taken into account, especially in the later periods.

Within the book's broad chronology, certain themes come to the fore according to the focus of different chapters: the division of labour and tension between craft and machine in the first chapter; modernism and the home in the second chapter; utility and warfare in the third chapter; shifting utopian and dystopian ideas that accompanied the discovery and spread of new materials and technologies in the post-war world of the fourth chapter; and the whole notion of 'good taste' in the fifth chapter. Throughout the book, we take the chair as an archetype of certain of these themes, showing how an item as basic and quotidian in its function has an apparently limitless variety of forms.

If a single, unifying issue drives the narrative it is the dynamic tension that existed, throughout the period in question, between two powerful ideas about the role of design. One is the link between design and the concept of taste: that the design of the objects and environments we choose forms and expresses our identities, and that this is the purpose of design. The other gives design a more idealistic agenda: we use design to improve the

In 1967 the French couturier Yves Saint Laurent introduced his collection of 'African' dresses, made from wooden beads, shells and raffia. This piece from the collection demonstrates the marriage Saint Laurent facilitated between the elegance of French haute couture and the naïve primitivism of the exotic source that inspired him.

quality of life through the thoughtful and responsible creation of designed objects that are widely accessible. This tension is lived out in the demise, in the late 1960s, of design modernism and the emergence, in its place, of design post-modernism. However, it is also present through the whole period, continually bubbling beneath the surface of design's progress and driving it forward. Indeed, as we move to the present day, and gaze into the future, it is clear that design, and designers, have to some extent come full circle. In addressing some of the big challenges that are affecting today's world – from over-production to climate change and financial challenges – William Morris's commitment to the political, social and ethical voices of design is, perhaps, more relevant today than it has ever been.

The Dutch designer Maarten Baas is associated with the radical Dutch group, named Droog (meaning 'dry'). His Hey Chair, Be a Bookshelf series, of 2005 is a typically challenging Baas design that made people look again. Each design is a seemingly arbitrary assemblage of familiar domestic items – a chair, a lampshade, a violin and a coat rack among them – all of them second-hand objects reinforced by polyester and coated by hand with polyurethane. It serves, in fact, to question the assumption that all products have a single function and cannot be used in other ways. In his creations a chair *can* become a bookshelf or a lampshade a vase.

MORE MATTER, WITH LESS ART

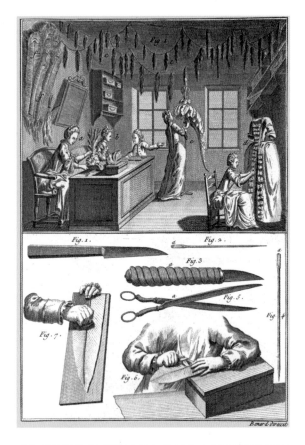

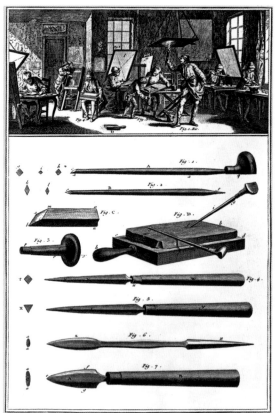

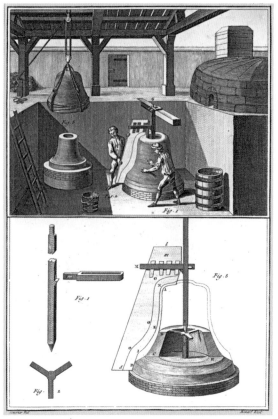

DESIGN AND INDUSTRY

From the minute we wake and turn off our alarm clocks to the moment we switch off our bedside lights at night we are so surrounded by design that it feels as if life must always have been lived this way. That is not so. Although the art of making things functional and beautiful has been part of our lives since the first cave walls were decorated and the first clay pot was thrown it wasn't until modern industrial manufacturing methods emerged in the eighteenth century that design took on the importance that it has for us today.

Design – as we know it now – is a modern phenomenon born of the radically new ways in which manufacturing was organised in the second half of the eighteenth century, starting in Great Britain and spreading to continental Europe and North America. Those 'new ways' were not simply the result of inventive production engineers developing processes and machines to make things more quickly, more cheaply and more efficiently for the sake of it, however; they were also a response to a dramatic increase in demand for goods by people who had never before been in a financial position to place aspiration above basic needs. The economic expansion of the 1750s onwards enabled those who had previously had to make do with relatively modest possessions – a few items of dress and some household textiles, ceramics and furniture – to seek to own goods that would make their lives more comfortable and also show off the enhanced social standing they sought for themselves. Manufacturers not only had to devise new products to meet these new demands, and to make them in greater numbers; they also had to ensure that these products were visually appealing and that their customers knew that they existed.

Inevitably not everybody was happy with this huge proliferation of goods. By the second half of the nineteenth century, an energetic reform campaign – championed most famously by William Morris and the Arts & Crafts Movement – had emerged to address what its followers believed had become the adverse effects of design's alliance with industry and mass production. This was the first appearance of a tension between a commercially oriented, consumer-focused approach to design and a more idealistic vision of the potential of design as a tool for social improvement. It is a tension that continues.

By the end of the nineteenth century another important theme of the alliance between design and industry had emerged. In contrast to the prevailing Victorian aesthetic of conspicuous flamboyance, designers such as Christopher Dresser in Britain, Peter Behrens in Germany and the architect-designer Frank Lloyd Wright in the US, focused on simplifying objects and environments to make them part of the modern world. The geometric, minimally decorated 'machine style' was the result of designers' determination to make factory-produced goods *look* like the products of a rational, mechanised process of manufacture.

The emergence of design between 1750 and 1900 results from three important factors: its links with industry; the role of the design reform movement; and the development of a modern machine style.

The textile industry was among the first to embrace mass production and the division of labour. Machine work undertaken by unskilled labourers replaced hand printing by skilled artisans. These new techniques produced textiles that were much cheaper whilst boasting patterns copied from more expensive fabrics. Design studio Timorous Beasties' London Toile **previous pages** playfully mimics hand-made, eighteenth-century French fabrics, using modern images, from muggings to Foster & Partner's Gherkin, alongside more traditional London views.

The four engraved images from Denis Diderot's *Encylopédie des Sciences et Métiers* (c. 1770) **opposite** show a range of craft workshops and the tools used by the skilled artisans working them during the period that preceded the advent of mechanisation and anonymous production. The feather workers **top left**; the engraving workshop **top right**; the paper marbler's workshop **bottom left**; and the image of bell casting **bottom right** all illustrate the makers' direct engagement with the materials at their disposal and the skilled use of their single-purpose tools.

Craft: art or industry

For centuries the rich acquired fashionable, decorative, hand-made objects through which to display their wealth and their social standing. The French philosopher, Denis Diderot, collected in his *Encyclopédie* (published between 1751 and 1772) many illustrations of these crafts (page 18). In eighteenth-century Britain the cabinet-makers Thomas Chippendale, George Hepplewhite and Thomas Sheraton provided furniture for those élite levels of society. Chippendale published his famous pattern book, *The Gentleman and Cabinet-Maker's Director*, in 1754 (page 24). With a preface by Samuel Johnson, it offered models for the hand-made furniture items that were made, on request, by Chippendale's craftsmen. Chippendale developed an acute sense of the prevailing tastes of the day. His shop in London's St Martin's Lane was a magnet for fashionable people and he offered them furniture in designs that fulfilled their aspirations. The contemporary French styles of Louis XV and Louis XVI with extravagant rococo curves predominated, but the astute furniture-maker went on to produce Gothic and Chinese styles for his wealthy customers, all cleverly adapted to fit the Anglo-Saxon temperament.

Chippendale worked with all his clients individually. His furniture pieces were made to order by his craftsmen. Nonetheless, his pattern book, models and London shop enabled him to market his work widely, and thus to sell and make as many pieces of furniture as possible. His 'business model' was on the cusp of what design and industry would soon adopt as normal practice. When the factories took over, making more goods available to more people, this model of product customisation did not disappear, however, but remained a common route through which the social and economic élite purchased their goods.

The Parisian fashion couturiers of the second half of the nineteenth century onwards worked exactly in this way to create unique gowns for their wealthy clients. Charles Frederick Worth, who was born in Lincolnshire but who worked in Paris from 1845 onwards, made lavish, one-off gowns for, among others, the French Empress Eugénie. Like Chippendale, he offered a range of designs which, in his case, could be individually made by his tailors on request. This traditional maker/client relationship continues to operate in parallel to factory production today. Indeed the processes of unique adaptation and hand-making have become – like the thrill of a ride in a customised car or of the purchase of an original pot from a craft fair today – a means by which people assert their individual identities by buying and displaying items that are themselves individual. Recently, flexible forms of manufacturing, made possible by high technology, are allowing unique products to be created at more accessible prices than ever before. The work of Michael Eden (page 28) is a good example of this.

Craft-making relies on the maker's tacit knowledge and skill, based on repeated practice, and involves chance and an ability to improvise. Factory production eliminated these elements. One way of understanding this shift is by comparing ceramic pots made on a wheel to others produced in moulds. Throwing pots involves implicit, un-articulated knowledge and a continual response by a skilled craftsman to the clay turning on the wheel, such that no two pots made in this way ever turn out exactly the same. By contrast, the design of pots made in moulds is predetermined, the knowledge of how to make them has to be explicit and they are more or less identical, their forms and surfaces created by the shape of the mould rather than directly by the craftsman's hand.

The Couturier's Workshop in Arles **opposite top**, painted by Antoine Raspal in 1760, shows a group of women hand-sewing clothes for aristocratic clients. Before the advent of the modern fashion system – which encouraged women from across the social spectrum to emulate those 'above them', and to renew their clothing in order to remain up to date – fashions lasted much longer. Gowns made of sumptuous fabrics with hand-made lace and other luxurious trimmings were prized possessions.

By the middle of the nineteenth century, Paris was established as the centre of couture fashion, and Charles Frederick Worth was one of the first designers to exploit the increasing interest in fashionable dress. Couture, such as this ballgown **left** from 1872, remained true to its hand-made origins, eschewing factory production, although Worth also presented his clients with pre-designed dresses that they could have made to their individual measurements.

The couturier remained the main supplier of expensive, custom-made dress through the first half of the twentieth century. Cecil Beaton's photograph of models in the neo-classical setting of Charles James's couture house (*Vogue*, June 1948) **opposite bottom** evokes the glamour and sophistication of couture in a composition remarkably similar to that of Raspal's painting.

Who makes what?

Design owes its existence to the entrepreneurial energies of the men who transformed Britain's manufacturing industries at the end of the eighteenth and the beginning of the nineteenth centuries. Britain was not, of course, the only country to embrace developments in manufacturing, as countries such as France had been active in finding new, efficient ways of producing goods, such as textiles, for some years. From 1804 onwards Joseph-Marie Jacquard had made a major contribution to the Lyon silk industry through the development of his new loom, but very few other industrial developments took place in nineteenth-century France, which remained a predominantly agricultural nation.

In the US, advances in modern manufacturing mostly occurred towards the end of the nineteenth century when the robber barons of the gilded age – Andrew Carnegie, John D. Rockefeller and Cornelius Vanderbilt – made huge steps forward in the industrialisation of the US. Britain's progress in this area took place at the end of the eighteenth century and through the early and middle nineteenth century and was hugely influential on the development of the modern concept of design as we know it today.

Specifically, design was a key by-product of the thinking that broke down the traditional, holistic craft process into its constituent elements and reconstructed them into a logical sequence of activities – in simple terms, designing, tooling, making individual components and assembling them. This thinking led to the possibility of manufacturing large numbers of cheap, identical goods. But mass production of identical goods at a low price required meticulous advance planning and considerable financial investment. Previously, design had been a spontaneous activity that occurred in an ad hoc manner as a craftsman worked intuitively with his material to create an object. Now, the process of making was a highly planned one, and the appearance of the finished object was complete before making even began: at the very outset of the manufacture of a product the designer had already decided on its appearance and how it was to be made.

Design was now of paramount importance – the designer less so. The idea of a single, highly skilled designer-maker was replaced by a manufacturing team made up of semi-skilled and unskilled workers who operated as part of a divided labour system. In the mass production of nineteenth-century ceramic objects, for example, no single person took on the role of the 'designer'. Rather, a number of different people were involved

The Jacquard loom **above** was one of the most technologically innovative factory machines. It transformed textile manufacture: the pre-determined design of the fabric was produced by holes punched in pattern cards which guided the loom – a form of binary programming that anticipates early computer codes.

Design embraces many practices, from fine art to engineering, and it is impossible to ignore the significance of highly skilled engineers who created the machines needed to power the factories, and without whom the Industrial Revolution could not have happened. James Watt's single acting steam engine, designed in the late eighteenth century, was illustrated in *Rees's Cyclopaedia* **right**, a publication that revealed the working of many of these new machines to an audience that was eager to participate in the excitement of the age. This particular engine was used for pumping at the Chelsea Water Works.

STEAM ENGINE.

Boulton and Watt's Engine on the original Construction.

Scale of Feet.

Elevation.

Plan of the Beam Floor.

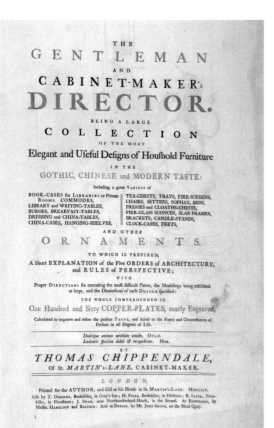

24

in the processes of creating prototypes and moulds. As the design historian, Adrian Forty, has explained in his book *Objects of Desire: Design and Society 1750–1980*, the specialised workman who prepared ceramic prototypes for mass production was called a 'modeller'. In the textile industry 'pattern-drawers', fairly lowly factory employees, who lacked the status of the fine artists employed in more upmarket production, were nevertheless important members of the design team. But as the design critic, John Gloag, has written, 'The designer was not regarded as a technician with authority. He was at best a pattern-maker, a malleable draftsman, the sort of man who could devise on his drawing board an infinity of variations on a theme. Machinery could stamp out machinery by the mile. All that was needed to set the machine at work were drawings.'

The machines used in the factories also exerted an influence on the final appearance of products, and prototypes had to be designed with the constraints of available production machinery in mind. However, the new machines, the technology they used and the resulting product could still be complex. The Jacquard loom – the mechanical precursor, in many ways, of the modern computer – was used in many forms of textile manufacturing and was fundamental to the succesful mass manufacture of the intricately patterned Paisley shawl. Like other machines it required the design of its products to be pre-programmed. Patterns were drawn on graph paper and handed to a worker who punched holes in cards that were used in the manufacturing process. As many as 424,000 cards could be used in a single shawl. Each hole corresponded to a hook on the loom that guided the warp thread so that the weft would lie either above or below it depending on the nature of the pattern that was required.

Designing for the market
One of the eighteenth century's most successful entrepreneurs, Josiah Wedgwood, was keen to use new production technologies, especially those linked to making ceramic items in moulds. He opened his first factory in Burslem in Staffordshire in 1759 in order to take advantage of the growing demand for domestic ceramics brought about by the expanded interest in tea- and coffee-drinking and the increasing popularity of hot cooked meals. His mass-produced, utilitarian cream-coloured earthenware, for example, proved a huge success. New industrial processes were introduced to make them, and new classes of pottery workers – mould designers and carvers among them – emerged to transfer their designs into mass production.

Wedgwood operated simultaneously on two levels, however, providing unique pieces for rich customers as well as his quantity-produced functional wares. He worked with a number of successful artists of the day, among them the sculptor John Flaxman and the painters Joseph Wright of Derby and George Stubbs, on products that targeted wealthy clients. Wedgwood would suggest the kind of work he wanted and the artists would design it, producing drawings, wax models, and occasionally plaster moulds. A series of Jasperware plaques depicting scenes from classical life (pages 26–7), as well as the famous Portland Vase, were among the many fruits of his close collaboration with Flaxman. Working with artists not only added value to his ornamental products but also, by association, to his utilitarian products. It enabled Wedgwood – as, today, it still does to makers such as the Italian company, Alessi – to manage the challenging tension between his desire to widen his market while still maintaining the social cachet of his designs. To succeed he also had to actively market his mass-produced wares.

Mass production depends on volume sales, and ever since the mid eighteenth century, savvy manufacturers and designers have used catalogues to publicise their ideas and sell their products **opposite**. Thomas Chippendale's *The Gentleman and Cabinetmaker's Director* from 1754 **top left** included 160 copper plates showing the stylistic virtuosity of this fashionable cabinetmaker. The architect and design reformer, Owen Jones, worked with Henry Cole on the Great Exhibition of 1851 and was intrumental in setting up what is now the V&A museum in London. Jones published *The Grammar of Ornament* (1856) to show, 'general principles in the arrangement of form and colour in architecture and the decorative arts', including these Egyptian motifs **top right**. Ingvar Kamprad, the founder of Ikea, published his first catalogue in 1951 **bottom left** and today prints more than 120 million copies of each new catalogue. That's a cost wholly avoided by mydeco **bottom right**, an online catalogue of furniture and homeware that arranges products in a magazine format according to styles and themes.

JOSIAH WEDGWOOD

One of the eighteenth century's most successful entrepreneurs, Josiah Wedgwood (1730-1795) **above** used design to add value to mass-produced earthenware and, at the top end of his range, to add social cachet to his products. He opened his first factory in Burslem, Staffordshire, in 1759 in order to meet the growing demand for domestic ceramics. The cream-coloured earthenware he mass produced **above right** was highly successful.

Wedgwood quickly realised that commercial opportunities existed to sell different products to different customers at a range of prices according to the design and production methods he used. Wedgwood joined forces with fine artists to create high-quality objects that were purely decorative, such as the Jasperware plate **above centre** with a relief designed by the artist John Flaxman. Wedgwood frequently collaborated with Flaxman, who would begin by drawing out a scene for later application as a relief. Many of the designs came from classical mythology: the drawing here **right** depicts Alcestis and Admetus.

Towards the end of his career, Wedgwood became obsessed with producing a Jasperware copy of what is known as the Portland Vase, a Roman antique blue-and-white glass vase from the first century BC. John Flaxman saw the original Roman vase and described it to Wedgwood as, 'the finest production of Art that has been brought to England and seems to be the very apex of perfection to which you are endeavouring.'

Wedgwood's Portland Vase **opposite** was a collaboration with Flaxman, and it took four years of painstaking attempts before they perfected its production in 1790. Earlier versions cracked or blistered; in others, the white relief lifted during firing. The first edition of 'perfect' copies went on show in a private exhibition, tickets to which had to be limited owing to the overwhelming interest – and the Vase marks Wedgwood's final great achievement.

The Wedgwood Portland Vase that is now in the V&A museum in London is thought to have come from the collection of Charles Darwin, Wedgwood's grandson.

A COMPOSITION FOR CHEAPNESS AND NOT EXCELLENCE OF WORKMANSHIP IS THE MOST FREQUENT AND CERTAIN CAUSE OF THE RAPID DECAY AND ENTIRE DESTRUCTION OF ARTS AND MANUFACTURES. – JOSIAH WEDGWOOD

Wedgwood's influence and legacy take many and various forms. Robert Dawson, of Robert Dawson Aesthetic Sabotage, overtly references Wedgwood's Chinese designs for his After Willow Pattern bone china platter, designed for Wedgwood in 2004 **right**.

Equally striking in its references to past ceramic production is work by the Dutch design group, Studio Job. Their biscuit porcelain Appearance plate (2006) **below right** combines traditional techniques with kitsch imagery, like this French poodle. The range was created for Royal Tichelaar Makkum, a Dutch ceramics company established over four hundred years ago.

Michael Eden's Wedgwoodn't tureen **below**, produced by Rapid Manufacture, acts as a commentary on the leaps and bounds that have taken place in the field of production technology since the eighteenth century, when Wedgwood introduced new machines into his Etruria factory. Eden's object uses new ceramic materials and is the result of rapid prototyping, a technique that can create a three-dimensional artefact from a two-dimensional drawing through a computerised process.

In complete contrast, the Dutch design group Studio Libertiny's honeycomb vase, Made by Bees (2007) **opposite**, was produced by what designer Tomas Gabzdil Libertiny calls 'slow prototyping'. A vase-shaped mould is placed into a hive and, over the course of a week, up to 40,000 bees do the rest of the work. Each vase is unique, and the final colour is determined by the flowers that are in season. 'The material comes from flowers as a by-product of bees, and in the form of a vase ends up serving flowers on their last journey,' Libertiny notes.

Marketing designs now became important because, while the economies of scale involved in mass-produced goods were clearly advantageous to the industrialist, there was a downside. Craft-made artefacts had a ready market – a more-or-less guaranteed sale to those who had commissioned them, but the potential consumers of the new factory-made goods did not know they wanted those particular items until they saw them in the marketplace. It also became part of the designer's job, therefore, to make products both visible and desirable. This fundamental transformation from craft to factory manufacturing, and the dramatic shift in the way goods were sold and bought, gave birth to the modern design process with which we are still familiar.

Selling designs

The divided labour system, and the isolation of 'designing' at the outset of the manufacturing process, underpinned the working procedures of many nineteenth-century firms producing goods for domestic consumption, from textiles

to ceramics to metalwork. Pictures of designs now began to play a significant role, both before and after manufacture. Matthew Boulton's Soho factory in Birmingham produced what were called 'toys', small metal items such as shoe buckles, tweezers, tooth picks, snuff boxes, inkstands and watch chains – which were manufactured in vast numbers. They were based on pattern-book models but modified by the specific production technologies that Boulton introduced into his factory. Pattern books became increasingly important: originating in Italy and Germany in the sixteenth century, these collections of engravings produced in quantity by the new mechanical printing methods were the main source of designs for factory-produced goods in the eighteenth century. By the 1770s they had been joined by illustrated trade catalogues, which promoted the goods in the marketplace.

Like Wedgwood, Boulton understood the selling power of art in products targeted at ordinary people as well as the social élite and, according to his biographer, H. W. Dickenson, 'For the purpose of obtaining designs for his products Boulton sought the aid of his friends in order through them to borrow works of art to act as models. The friends in question were mostly fashionable fine artists of the day.' Again, like Wedgwood, Boulton understood the need for intensive marketing when launching designs in order to recoup the manufacturer's capital investment. One vital role of design was to make the goods in the marketplace appeal to potential customers by reflecting their desires and aspirations.

From the end of the eighteenth century on, as the amount of factory-produced goods increased, so there was an increase in the number of shops in which to buy them. Paris saw the establishment of its first *grand magasin* – La Belle Jardinière – in 1824, which was followed by the Bon Marché store just over a decade later. Alexander Turney Stewart built his Marble Palace dry goods store in New York City in 1848 while London also became a commercial centre of note and many new shops – from Fortnum & Mason to Heal's – were established. The role of the travelling salesman was also intensified as manufacturers had to work harder and harder to sell their goods.

The innovations developed by the new industries focused, therefore, on the divided labour system; on the identification and isolation of the design process as a distinct, and early, element within that system; on the realisation that a more aggressive approach towards marketing and selling needed to be developed; and on the self-conscious addition of art to distinguish goods. While production was the tail that wagged the dog it was, of necessity, closely linked to the rules that governed consumption. Design emerged as we know it today: an activity separate – for the first time – from making, and necessary before making could begin. Design was also a process that, if done well, added value to the goods produced – that is, it gave them a competitive lead in the marketplace.

A coloured lithograph published by Dickenson Brother **opposite** of the hardware exhibit at the Exhibition of all Nations, held in London's Hyde Park in 1851. The image conveys a strong sense of the abundance of goods on display at that popular event and the way in which the eyes of the visitors were bombarded by the plethora of objects presented to them.

By contrast, the 1951 Festival of Britain was a more restrained affair. It was dominated by the futuristic architecture of Ralph Tubbs's Dome of Discovery and its dramatic engineered features **above**. Once inside the Festival pavilions, however, the audience enountered rich displays that led them through Britain's achievements over the last century and gave them a taste of the technologically led future that, it was believed, lay in front of them.

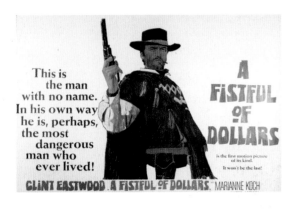

Conspicuous consumption

While factory production, and the presence of more and more goods in the everyday environment, brought a great deal of pleasure, especially to those who had not been able to buy luxury items before, it also had its critics. The *Great Exhibition of the Works of Industry of All Nations*, conceived by Prince Albert and Henry Cole, the arts administrator and exhibition director, and held in London's Hyde Park in 1851, was the trigger for many of them to express their views. The purpose of the exhibition was to demonstrate the strengths of British production in an international setting. The huge glass-and-steel building created for the event was designed by Joseph Paxton and, because of the amount of glass in its manufacture, was quickly dubbed 'the Crystal Palace'. For those such as the art critic John Ruskin and the designer William Morris, who were to lead the nineteenth-century reform movement – which, in its turn, was to set in motion the twentieth-century modern movement in design – the 1851 exhibition represented everything that was wrong with the goods that flowed from the factories and which targeted nouveau-riche consumers. The design of these goods was separated from their manufacture, and their over-ornamentation flouted the craft-based principles of 'truth to materials', flagrantly ignoring the principles of 'fitness for purpose' and 'form follows function'. For Ruskin, Morris and many others the flamboyant items of furniture, metalwork, ceramics and glass that were shown in the Crystal Palace reflected the lack of taste of consumers with newly acquired wealth.

In his 1937 retrospective account of the 1851 Exhibition Christopher Hobhouse described the abundance of textiles displayed there, giving an indication of the level of rich extravagance on view. 'There are', he wrote, 'plush and brocade and bombazeen and moiré and taffetas and tabinet and lutestring and poplin and sarsnet and gossamer and gauze; and there are veils and Berthas and silk hats and fishing lines and silk whips and chenilles and galloons. It was a period that took a sensual pleasure in stuffs, when fifty guineas worth of silk were cut to swing and rustle round a single pair of legs.' The sense of material opulence and conspicuousness that is evocatively described here pervaded the whole event. In another very telling statement Hobhouse emphasised the appeal of exotic materials. 'To the Victorians,' he wrote, 'who were very apt to judge of beauty by the amount of labour that had gone into its making, malachite offered an irresistible appeal.' Extravagant decoration was considered beautiful because it revealed the amount of work that had been undertaken to achieve it and because its rich texture and origins evoked an exotic world. The fact that that work could now be done by a team of unskilled or semi-skilled workers, very probably working with machines, rather than by the hand of a skilled craftsman, was not a problem for the new consumers. What mattered to them was that, for the first time, they could own, or aspire to own, a plethora of richly

The simple form of the Colt Navy revolver (c. 1851) **bottom left** is a result of its rational production from standardised, interchangeable components and the fact that it is essentially a utilitarian object with a single function – to kill. However, the addition of the small amount of stamped decoration on some of its metal elements indicates that even this killing machine contains a level of decorative expression that defines it as an aesthetic artefact as well, albeit minimally. Colt's revolvers ranged, in fact, from objects of pure utility to ceremonial totems that had quite another function.

The basic revolver remains a powerful icon, as the poster for *A Fistful of Dollars* (1964) **top left** illustrates, showing Clint Eastwood holding a Colt 45 in his right hand with its trigger cocked, ready to shoot and kill. The mass-produced revolver by the American Colt company was among the first standardised products made of interchangeable parts to come out of an American factory. The new production system responded to the US military's need for the rapid repair of broken weapons with replacement parts that could be fitted at speed.

Engineers played an important role in the creation of the modern environment of the nineteenth century. Isambard Kingdom Brunel was one of Britain's most productive and radical engineers. His Royal Albert Bridge (1859) **above**, built to cross the River Tamar at Saltash in Cornwall, uses wrought-iron trusses that enabled Brunel to span a distance of 142 metres/465 feet and to create a lasting image of nineteenth-century ambition and inventiveness.

decorated objects that acted as visual markers of their newly acquired social status and taste. For the reformers, however, design had gone bad.

Taste

In the mid nineteenth century the notion of taste was understood as an absolute, rather than a relative, concept. There was no 'good' or 'bad' taste, simply taste. Moreover it was invested with considerable social and cultural significance. The possession of taste distinguished someone with social cachet from someone without it. But for nouveau-riche consumers, taste was often synonymous with complexity and abundance. As John Gloag has explained, 'Victorian taste was confused by the belief that ornament and design were identical and was profoundly influenced by a secret religion, to which men and women occasionally gave not their souls, but their bodies: the religion of comfort.' The mid-century parlour reflected this attitude at its most extreme. Filled with a plethora of richly decorated artefacts – furniture, textiles on any and every surface, stuffed birds in glass domes, aspidistras, ceramics and glass objects, photographs in decorative frames, patterned carpets and wallpapers and trinkets of all sorts – it offered comfort through the deep upholstery on its sofas and chairs, and the softening of its hard surfaces with a range of textiles.

Magnificent steamships, bridges, viaducts and other wonderful feats of engineering, undertaken by men such as Isambard Kingdom Brunel, as well as impressive architecture – exemplified by the Palace of Westminster and St. Pancras Station in Britain and in France by the work of the architect, Viollet-le-Duc – characterise the Victorian age and its material achievements. However, it was the highly decorated domestic parlour and its contents that inspired the discussion about taste that was to dominate debates about design in the second half of the nineteenth century – and indeed beyond. The same debate went on to stimulate the later modern movement in design and its progress through the twentieth and into the twenty-first centuries. Many critics, both within the period and subsequently, have frequently voiced their anxieties about the excesses and the false values that they believed characterised the Victorian parlour. From that debate emerged a set of principles that by the middle of the twentieth century had come to define, and indeed continue to define, the idea of 'good design'.

The early reformers

While nouveau-riche consumers delighted in the rich decoration of the domestic parlour, the design reformers associated it with unbridled mass production and conspicuousness and deeply regretted the dismantling of the link between designing and making. The nineteenth-century debate about taste was initiated by a group of individuals from the worlds of architecture and fine art who were highly critical of the designed goods that flowed from the newly constructed factories. William Morris was to develop his radical and highly influential ideas on the harmful effects on society of the division of labour and the mechanisation of production, but a few decades before this, the architect A. W. N. Pugin and the artist, writer and critic John Ruskin had already expressed their views about the effects of industrialisation on the material world. Pugin's response to its perceived 'evils', which he expressed in his 1836 book *Contrasts* and in his publication of 1841, *The Principles of Pointed or Christian Architecture*, was a plea to return to the craft-based medieval world, and the spiritual purity of Gothic architecture and design. Ruskin shared Pugin's commitment to medievalism.

John Everett Millais' painting of the writer and critic, John Ruskin (1853), places him at the rocky edge of a cascading waterfall – in the uncontrollable world of nature that was so important to him. The awe and wonder that Ruskin felt as he contemplated the natural world permeated all his work, as did his strong religious commitment. Millais (who later married Ruskin's former wife) presents the forces of nature in an ambiguous relationship to Ruskin, who is painted as an archetypally modern man. Millais carefully renders Ruskin's facial features and clothes in a realist style that embodies Ruskin's commitment to detail and truthful representation.

WILLIAM MORRIS

The work of William Morris (1834-96) is so instantly recognisable today that it can be difficult to imagine the shock and impact it had in the nineteenth century. Morris is often romanticised, when in fact he was a radical, and his work has become a byword for 'good taste', when it was not alway so. Frederick Hollyer's portrait photograph of Morris **above** captures his sitter's earnestness. Morris looked backwards (to the medieval world) as well as forwards, and led a movement in design that aimed to reinstate the joy in work that, he believed, had existed before the advent of factories, as well as the link between making and the well-being of society that characterised the pre-industrial world.

Following his marriage to Jane Burden in 1859, Morris embarked upon the building of a house for his new family in partnership with the architect, Philip Webb. The Red House in Bexleyheath, Kent (1859) **above right**, contains overtly medieval references, expressed by the pointed arches over the windows and the entrance arch. As such, it reflects Morris's view that in the medieval world the craftsman had worked in tune with society and that his own products had established a link between making and using that had been lost within the division of labour. At the same time, the use of red brick without stucco was a startling departure from Victorian norms.

The vertical, tapered newel posts on the oak staircase **left** reinforce the medievalism of the Red House, as do the bold geometric patterns on the ceilings. Morris invited his Pre-Raphaelite colleagues to contribute to the interior decoration of his home. They added medieval-style patterns to many of its structural surfaces and also decorated a number of furniture items, whilst Morris included some of his own textile and furniture designs.

Morris's Rose textile (1883) **right** is composed of flowers, leaves, stems and birds in a relatively complex pattern. However, the stylisation of the imagery, the controlled repeats and the flat background ensure that the two dimensions of the surface are not denied, realising Morris's commitment to 'truth to materials'.

THE PAST IS NOT DEAD; IT IS LIVING IN US, AND WILL BE ALIVE IN THE FUTURE WHICH WE ARE NOW HELPING TO MAKE. – WILLIAM MORRIS

Karen Hsu and Michael Rock of 2x4 in New York produced this floral collage of cropped and pixelated imagery culled from videos **left** as an installation for the Prada Epicenter store in New York, designed by OMA/Rem Koolhaas in 2001. Their Prada Vomit wallpaper harks back to and links Morris's late nineteenth-century world to the present. Production techniques may have changed but the desire to use images from the natural world – and to cover the surfaces of our interior spaces with patterns – is alive and well.

More than 100 years after his death, William Morris has become a leading brand of the so-called heritage industry. The fabric of this Seaweed deckchair **above** has been copied from a 1901 woodblock wallpaper. It can be bought at the V&A museum shop, along with umbrellas, bags and other gewgaws sporting Morris & Co. designed patterns.

Ruskin also shared Pugin's dedication to the world of nature and expressed his ideas in a number of texts including *The Seven Lamps of Architecture* (1849) and *The Stones of Venice* (1851–3). Both men embraced the idea of ornament but believed that, in the words of Ruskin, it should be 'visible, natural and thoughtful'. For Ruskin the evils of mechanised mass production were epitomised in the displays at the Crystal Palace, which he disparagingly dubbed 'a greenhouse larger than greenhouse was ever built before'.

Other mid-Victorian reformers wanted to inform designers and improve public taste through example and education, and lobbied for institutions in which to do this. In 1824 Sir Robert Peel established the National Gallery in order to 'instil a sense of design in the manufacturer and … elevate taste in the consumer', while 1837 witnessed the opening of the first government school of design in South Kensington (now the Royal College of Art), which was followed by the creation of many others located in industrial centres throughout England and Scotland. In 1847 Henry Cole and other influential reformers formed 'Summerly's Art Manufactures' in order to 'put fine art at the service of manufactured objects', while two years later the group published the *Journal of Art Manufactures* to further their efforts to improve the standards of taste in British manufactured goods.

Design with a moral purpose

That design could be more than a question of personal taste – that it could have social as well as political implications – was an argument most famously championed by the best-known design reformer of all: William Morris. Like those of many of his reforming colleagues his early thoughts about design were stimulated by his exposure to the 1851 exhibition. While he saw the problem as industrial manufacture he was not, as is often suggested, against the use of the machine per se. 'It is not', he clearly wrote, 'this or that tangible steel or brass machine which we want to get rid of, but the great intangible machine of commercial tyranny which oppresses the lives of all of us.' For Morris, like Karl Marx before him, the division of labour lay at the heart of the problem, as he believed that it had led to alienation in work and to the production and consumption of what he considered to be inappropriate ornament. For Morris, unlike Marx, however, that alienation resulted not only in the despicable exploitation of the working class but also in what he considered to be the overly bright, coloured patterns on a carpet on a parlour floor.

Indeed, for many of the design critics, using nature as a source of pattern on the surface of textiles, such as carpets, and giving the impression that one was walking on real flowers, was the ultimate design crime. You could not just, for example, apply a picture of a plant to a surface; you had to consider the object being so decorated – what was appropriate, how the decoration fitted with the function of the object and the very lines of the ornamentation should be the product of a design *choice*, not mere imitation. It is ironic that, today, Morris's textile and wallpaper designs are seen largely as decorative whereas their patterns derive from the rigorous application of a design ethos.

In 1856 the design reformer Owen Jones wrote in his influential book, *The Grammar of Ornament*, that 'flowers or natural objects should not be used as ornaments, but conventional representations founded upon them sufficiently suggestive to convey the intended image to the mind, without destroying the unity of the object they are employed to decorate'. Four decades later the designer and reformer Lewis F. Day was also to

Published in 1896, William Morris's Kelmscott Chaucer is widely recognised as the finest publication of the Arts & Crafts Movement. Morris specially designed the medieval-style Chaucer font, lavish ornamental borders and decorative capitals to complement woodcut illustrations by Edward Burne-Jones, who declined to illustrate some of the racier scenes from Chaucer's *Canterbury Tales*.

'If we live to finish it, it will be like a pocket cathedral,' Burne-Jones declared. After four years of labour, it was published just months before Morris's death in October 1896.

write, 'One can scarcely conceive of ornament which is not, in a manner, more or less modified by considerations altogether apart from the natural forms on which it may have been founded.' In other words, direct copying from nature was wrong and designers needed a more subtle understanding of the relation between ornament and the object being ornamented.

From the 1860s Morris's writings and work also focused on the need to control ornament. Like Ruskin, on whose ideas he depended heavily, Morris embraced medievalism and believed that ornament should express nature appropriately. 'What we call decoration is,' he explained, 'in many cases, but a way we have learned for making necessary things reasonable as well as pleasant to use. The pattern becomes a part of the thing we make, its exponent, a mode of expressing itself to us, and by it we often form our own opinions not only of the shape, but of the strength and uses of the thing.' Morris's ideas helped define modern design. He believed that decoration should not be understood as an add-on, linked to social status, but rather as an intrinsic, defining property of objects, communicating their functions and their identities to their users. In this respect William Morris was, as Nikolaus Pevsner was later to describe him, a true pioneer of modern design.

Morris exemplified what he meant by good design in his home, the Red House in Bexleyheath, which was conceived by his friend Philip Webb in 1859. Because he could not find anything he wanted to fit it out with in the shops, he and his friends in the Arts & Crafts Movement made the furnishings of the house, and it had decoration by the Pre-Raphaelite painters, Dante Gabriel Rossetti, Ford Madox Brown and Edward Burne-Jones. Morris formed a furniture and decorative arts firm, eventually known as Morris & Co., and during the 1860s and 1870s he became known for his designs for textiles, wallpapers and carpets which testified to his skills as a master pattern-maker. His last years were dedicated to printing, as well as to embroidery and tapestry, and the highly influential books and typefaces he designed for the Kelmscott Press were inspired by medieval manuscripts. Morris's wallpapers and textiles are still in quantity production over a hundred years after his death.

While Morris's subtle adaptations of natural forms – flowers, leaves and birds among them – to the demands of two dimensions led to his longstanding success as a designer, his political ideas were also vitally important to the influence he exerted on the course of modern design. In essence he sought to retain the joy in making that he believed had characterised the work of the medieval craftsman. 'Nothing should be made by man's labour,' he wrote, 'which is not worth making or which must be made by labour degrading to the maker.' In essence he sought to maintain an ethical link between production and consumption. If things were made with joy they would, he believed, also be used with joy.

Morris's legacy to modern design is ultimately double-edged, however. While, on the one hand, he sought to democratise design – 'I don't want art for a few, any more than education for a few, or freedom for a few,' he famously declared – he found it difficult to run a successful business without the work his firm undertook for wealthy clients. He is remembered ultimately, however, for the radical simplicity and humanism of his designs and for his understanding of the need to stylise and make nature abstract in the process of pattern-making. His commitment to the tenets of 'truth to materials' and 'fitness to purpose' offered a modern approach to design that was to find its ultimate expression in the twentieth-century modern movement.

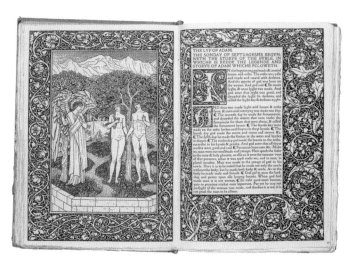

Back to the future

Like Morris, many of the other Arts & Crafts protagonists also gazed simultaneously backwards and forwards. They created medieval-style guilds – Mackmurdo's Century Guild, formed in 1882; Lethaby and Crane's Art Workers' Guild (which included Morris), formed in 1884; and C.R. Ashbee's Guild and School of Handicraft, formed in 1888, among them. However they also embraced the machine, if properly used. 'Modern civilisation rests on machinery,' explained Ashbee, 'and no system for the endowment or encouragement of the teaching of art can be sound that does not recognise this.' Ultimately, however, their work – from W.A.S. Benson's strikingly contemporary-looking metal objects and C.F.A. Voysey's spare interiors to Ashbee's elegant jewellery – took design forward into the modern age. Their graceful, uncluttered lines reflected a commitment to the idea that Victorian excess needed to be replaced by a new aesthetic of simplicity and honesty.

The rise of the machines

The group of reformers around Henry Cole were more impressed by the sections of the 1851 Exhibition dedicated to machines than they were to the decorative art objects displayed there. Indeed, in many ways, the real design achievements of the Victorians were their remarkable engineering structures – the bridges, railways stations and industrial buildings that they created – and it was to them that the heroes of the modern movement – Le Corbusier, Walter Gropius and Mies Van der Rohe among them – looked for inspiration. For the architectural modernist architects and designers of the first decades of the twentieth century it was the machine that defined the modern age. Le Corbusier was famously to call the house 'a machine for living in'.

The application of a rational, undecorated aesthetic to consumer goods and machines – from furniture to typewriters to automobiles to computers – became a dominant feature of the first half of the twentieth century; but it was not an automatic consequence of mechanisation and it took some time for designers to create it. Initially the appearance of machines and their products was designed merely so that their parts fitted together and they worked efficiently; or decoration could be applied superficially, for example to make them fit in a domestic setting; or the designer could make a conscious effort to embrace their modernity and to use design to communicate the function of the object. In this progression of design, the US led the way.

America's industrialisation programme had, like that of Europe, originally lagged behind Britain's, but it quickly caught up and, where the introduction of machines was concerned, had overtaken Britain by the end of the nineteenth century, as a result of the US's shortage of manpower. The main impetus behind this was the rapid emergence of an increasingly affluent, highly homogeneous American mass market.

The first sewing machines to come off factory production lines in the 1860s were crude objects that resembled industrial rather than domestic machinery. This lockstitch machine **above**, produced by the Wheeler and Wilson Manufacturing Company based in Bridgeport, Connecticut, is made from a combination of wood, cast iron, steel and wrought iron and must have looked completely out of place in a decorated, nineteenth-century, middle-class parlour.

Domestic and office machines also took on modern visual identities in the early twentieth century as manufacturers brought in industrial designers to 'style' them. The German AEG company was among the first to understand the importance of integrating its products into a coherent corporate identity. The modernity of its Olympia typewriter is reinforced by the diagonal lines and progressive typography in this 1935 advertisement **right**.

ENFIN J'AI UNE

AEG Olympia

....RAPIDE SOLIDE, PRÉCISE

HENRY FORD

Along with Wedgwood the other great hero of the Industrial Revolution was the American automobile manufacturer, Henry Ford (1863-1947). While Wedgwood understood the need for mass-produced utility ware, Ford introduced a new factory system that featured the moving assembly line, enabling him to produce his Model T (**above** with Ford in Buffalo, NJ, in 1921) in vast quanties.

Ford's main innovation in industrial manufacturing was the moving assembly line, inspired by the meat-packing industry based in Chicago, where carcasses hung on moving lines while the 'disassemblers' stood still. Employees of the Chicago firm, Swift & Co. **above right** are shown in around 1908, splitting backbones and giving hog carcasses a final inspection before they were sent off for refrigeration.

In 1909 Ford took the decision to manufacture only one type of car, the Model T **below right**. Initially it took 14 hours to assemble a Model T. By improving his mass-production methods, Ford reduced this to one hour 33 minutes, lowering the overall cost of each car and enabling Ford to undercut the price of others on the market. Between 1908 and 1916 the selling price of the Model T fell from $1,000 to $360.

By the early 1920s the demand for cheap cars required Ford to move to a new, larger factory where production was intensified. As the engines passed by them each worker added a single component.

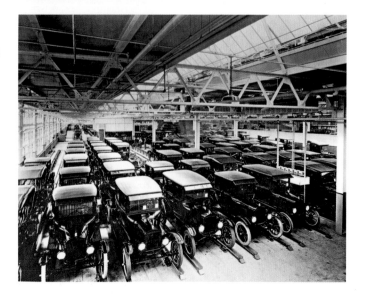

The inflexibility of Ford's highly rationalised production system proved his undoing, however, and at the end of the 1920s, he had to close the River Rouge factory for a year in order to create a new automobile that would compete with General Motors' more stylish products. Production at the Ypsilanti plant **above** resumed in 1930, by which time GM's Chevrolet was the best-selling car in America.

This market consumed standardised factory-made products as quickly as they could be produced. From the outset, learning from its arms industry and later its meat-packing industry, the US developed a highly rationalised mass-production system based on the principles of product standardisation, the interchangeability of parts, mechanisation and, eventually, the moving assembly line. What came to be called 'the American system of manufacture' was to play an important part in the story of modern design.

The very first consumer products manufactured in America looked crude. Singer's 1851 sewing machine, for example, was undecorated and highly utilitarian in appearance and the housewife used the wooden packing case it arrived in as a sewing table. It was not long, however, before the company realised that, while a housewife might be willing to buy a visually unsophisticated object as her first sewing machine, when she came to replace it she was more likely to buy one with decoration on its surface that would match her other domestic possessions. She would also prefer to place it on a polished wooden table that blended with her other furniture. The first suction sweeper produced by the Hoover Company in the early twentieth century, with its broom handle, visible rivets and separate dust bag, was another domestic product that looked as if it had merely come off an assembly line. In an attempt to redress that impression, a purple art nouveau pattern was quickly applied to the surface of its metal body shell to ensure that it didn't look out of place in a home. (Whereas in Britain cleaning objects were most likely to be bought for use by servants, in the US servants were in short supply and the suction sweeper was more likely to be bought and used by the housewife herself, reinforcing the need for added decoration). Even early typewriters, although located in offices rather than the home, displayed decoration on their surfaces because they were mostly used by women. Indeed women were keen to reproduce their domestic settings in the workplace and often introduced decorative features, such as pictures and Oriental fans, into them.

Designing the competitive edge

The design of the early twentieth-century, mass-produced automobile tells a similar story to that of the early sewing machine: one of an unselfconscious factory aesthetic being rapidly overtaken by the application of a conscious style that reflected consumer desire. In around 1912 Henry Ford pioneered the fully fledged model of mass production that combined divided labour, product standardisation, interchangeable parts, mechanisation and a moving assembly line. The 'Model T' Ford was a very basic car that eschewed luxury. Its appeal lay in its price and its efficiency, rather than in its appearance. Its success, however, like that of the first crudely designed Singer sewing machine, was relatively short-lived. In the 1920s, when Ford had moved to his expanded River Rouge factory, it quickly became apparent that the more stylish automobiles manufactured by his competitor, General Motors, were stealing the market from him, and he realised that he would have to update his product. Consumers had been willing to buy their first car on the basis of its price and utility alone. When it came to replacing it with a second car there was more competition around, including the second-hand car market, and consumers, who were by those years more urban, wealthy and sophisticated, looked for a form of added value in their automobiles. They found it in the visual variety offered by General Motors which kept its lines – Cadillac, Buick, Pontiac and

The assembly line remains part of the contemporary industrial landscape. Edward Burtynski's photograph, Manufacturing no. 17 (2005) **previous pages**, depicts a view across the Deda chicken processing plant in Dehui City, Jilin Provence, China: a sea of anonymous, unskilled workers undertaking similarly tedious, repetitive tasks to those of Ford's employees eighty years earlier.

The 1920s and 1930s saw the box-like, utilitarian automobile transformed into a curved, sensuous object of desire – a dream machine that bore little resemblance to its visually uninspiring predecessor. The contribution, from the late 1920s to the 1950s, of the first car stylist, Harley Earl, at General Motors helped bring about this transformation. 'Getting into a car should be like going on holiday,' explained Earl. The 1904 Buick **opposite top left** has little to differentiate it from an early Ford, but by 1927 this Buick Lasalle V8 with Harley Earl at the wheel **top right** had introduced elements of style to create an object of desire. The use of design to differentiate products, and to create a 'new model' every year helped General Motors sustain a demand for its products, including: a 1939 Buick 80 Roadmaster **middle left**; a 1942 Pontiac **middle right**; a 1949 Buick **bottom left**; and a 1957 Cadillac Coupe de Ville **bottom right**.

I WILL BUILD A CAR FOR THE GREAT MULTITUDE. IT WILL BE CONSTRUCTED OF THE BEST MATERIALS, BY THE BEST MEN TO BE HIRED, AFTER THE SIMPLEST DESIGNS THAT MODERN ENGINEERING CAN DEVISE. BUT IT WILL BE SO LOW IN PRICE THAT NO MAN MAKING A GOOD SALARY WILL BE UNABLE TO OWN ONE. – HENRY FORD

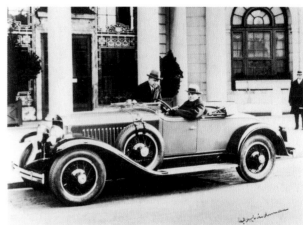

Richard Riemerschmid's little walnut chair from 1899 **above** is cleverly designed to include a diagonal element that supports the whole structure and leaves the seat open. Its simple form was characteristic of Deutscher Werkbund designs of the early twentieth century.

A poster, designed by Fritz Hellmuth Ehmcke, advertises the Deutscher Werkbund's 1914 exhibition in Cologne **right**. It was here that Henry van de Velde and Herman Muthesius locked horns in a lively debate about the importance of individualism or standardisation in design for mass production.

Chevrolet among them – quite distinct from each other, each one appealing to a different social grouping. In order to be able to benefit from the economies of scale of mass production, General Motors utilised a common chassis but it introduced different surface colours and trim to differentiate the various lines. While its production process was rationalised to a considerable extent, an awareness of the tastes and desires of the market, and a strategic use of design, enabled the company to overtake Ford in the 1920s.

The further aesthetic shift that took place in early twentieth-century products – the shift from their design being linked to surface decoration to its becoming an integral part of their form and identity – is one of the most important stylistic transformations in the story of modern design. There was no direct, natural flow from mechanised production to the emergence of 'machine-styled' products as one might have expected, however. Rather it was the result of the work of a couple of generations of forward-looking designers who took their cue from contemporary architecture and fine art – which had been quicker to respond to the exciting new forms and cultural possibilities of the machine age – and applied them back to the same factory-made products that had inspired the architects and artists in the first place.

Simplicity and standardisation

The work of British Arts & Crafts architects and designers, such as Christopher Dresser, sought to simplify objects and reflect the nature of their materials in their designs. Many, and Dresser in particular, were inspired by the simple objects emerging from Japan towards the end of the nineteenth century. It was in Germany, however, in the first decade of the twentieth century, that real innovation occurred in design with the emergence of the self-conscious machine style, proclaiming itself as the aesthetic for modern consumer goods and machines. The work of the Deustcher Werkbund, founded in 1907, was central to that achievement. Comprising manufacturers, retailers, politicians, architects and designers, this group was the first to apply the rationality of the machine to the products of mass production. Following the Arts & Crafts designers, its main tenets were that form should only be determined by function, and that decoration by ornamentation be eliminated. Designers such as Richard Riemerschmid and Bruno Paul pioneered the manufacture of very simple, standardised, machine-made furniture items, while the radical programme of designs that Peter Behrens created for the German AEG company consolidated the arrival of the twentieth-century modern machine style in the world of consumer goods. As well as taking product design forward, however, Behrens' work for AEG was also an early exercise in corporate identity. In the late nineteenth century, American companies and their designers had done a lot of work in the highly commercial fields of packaging and branding. Kellogg's cornflakes, Coca-Cola, Quaker Oats, Colgate toothpaste, Nabisco biscuits, Heinz pickles, Wrigley's chewing gum and Gillette razors had all developed strong brand identities. At AEG, Behrens took that work one step further by creating a single design language that united the company's graphics with its factory buildings and its products. Together they formed a distinctive, highly unified identity that made a huge impact in the marketplace.

At the Werkbund's 1914 exhibition in Cologne a debate broke out between the architect Hermann Muthesius, who supported standardized design, and the Belgian Art Nouveau architect and designer, Henry van der Velde, who defended individual artistic expression. The debate that ensued was

symptomatic of a fundamental tension that existed in design at that time, one that was to underpin discussions about the principles of 'good design' through the twentieth century. In the end, the Werkbund moved design towards Muthesius's standardised, collective approach. Although the First World War was to create a hiatus in the immediate development of those ideas, they surfaced again in the 1920s both in Germany and elsewhere in Europe.

The industrial designer

The late 1920s saga of Ford versus General Motors, is hugely significant for the story of modern design. It served to shift design's centre of gravity from production to consumption and from needs to wants. General Motors' employment of the automotive stylist Harley Earl – a former Hollywood custom-car designer – demonstrated that, as Wedgwood had realised a century earlier, while designers were important to the production process, in creating goods that would sell they were even more crucial. As his famous statement that a car could be any colour, 'as long as it's black' clearly indicated, Ford had believed that differences in design would be unimportant to the consumer; cars could look identical and this extreme standardisation underpinned the highly rationalised production system he introduced. The cars that rolled off the assembly lines looked, in the earlier words of the economist Adam Smith, as 'alike as two pins'.

General Motors president Alfred Sloan's appointment of Harley Earl in 1927 as head of the newly created Art and Colour – later Style – section changed all that. The hugely influential Earl pioneered car design, with hundreds of innovations from tail-fins to wraparound windscreens, iconic cars from the Firebird to the Corvette, and introduced the idea of the concept car or prototype. The consumer-focused definition of design developed by General Motors was bought into by many companies from the 1920s onwards. Harley Earl's success led to the emergence of the American consultant industrial design profession that reached its peak of influence in the 1930s; it took many visual ideas from Europe but applied them to the new consumer machines in the highly commercial context of the US. In the process American designers helped create a new, mid-twentieth-century modern material landscape. The idea of consultant designers for industry continues to exist today, emphasising the need for design to connect production with consumption.

By the early twentieth century the concept of design, as we now understand it, was fully formed. It was a clearly defined activity isolated from the rest of the manufacturing process; it was the component of goods that linked production and consumption – that indeed helped ensure consumption after production; and it embodied the modern world. If we were asked to think about what defines the age we live in, most of us would conjure up the images, objects, goods, clothes, buildings and other environments that modern design has produced.

By the early twenty-first century, design's relationship with manufacturing remains as strong as ever. The changing nature of production has inevitably meant, however, that this relationship has constantly evolved. Many models of mechanised manufacture – from high-volume to low-volume production to 'rapid manufacturing' – co-exist in today's world. Sometimes manufacturers call the tune, at others designers take the lead. Above all, though, the concept of design is still inextricably linked to industrial manufacture and that relationship is likely to continue.

A number of fine artists were inspired by the dramatic forms and the scale of factory machines in the first half of the twentieth century. The Mexican painter, Diego Rivera, was among those who saw machinery as representing the victory of technology that underpinned cultural modernism. His massive fresco *Detroit Industry* (1932-3) was commissioned by Edsel Ford, President of the Ford Motor Company, and William Valentiner, Director of the Detroit Institute of Arts. It emphasised man's vulnerability in the face of the new machines offset by the power of his intellect in having created them. In its entirety, the mural covers two walls to represent the races that shape North American culture and make up its work force, the automobile industry and the other industries of Detroit (medical, pharmaceutical, and chemical).

THE CHAIR: HIGH STYLING

In both form and function, the chair is a fairly basic object: it has a seat, usually at a height above the floor that is commonly in proportion to the adult human; four legs (usually); a back at something between 90 degrees and 100 degrees to the seat; and sometimes two arms. It is so intrinsically related to its function and to human needs that its parts – seat, arms, legs – share their names with human anatomy.

In spite – or perhaps because – of this, designers and architects seem endlessly facinated by chairs. Historically, chairs have been styled according to prevailing notions of taste; indeed, up until the Renaissance, the chair was a sign of social status and an emblem of authority.

The chair underwent several face-lifts in its journey from the eighteenth century, through the nineteenth century and into the late twentieth century. Chippendale's classic, French-influenced side chair **right** is but one of many designs that he adapted, in a wide range of styles, from rococo to Gothic and Chinoiserie in anticipation of his customer's preferences.

Robert Venturi's irreverent, postmodern Chippendale chair for Knoll International (1984) **top** is part of a series of nine chairs that he designed as an exploration of American and European furniture history. The almost clichéd simplication of form and the use of plywood and veneer make the chair, on one level, a design 'joke', juxtaposing historical reference with contemporary knowing.

Philipp Starck's transparent, Louis XV-inspired Ghost chair for Kartell (2005) **left** is made from polycarbonate in a single mould, a feat of technology unthinkable even 10 years ago. Its appearance is partly a reference to historical style but equally a response to manufacturing technology.

The use of embellishment to create difference and add value is not unique to named designers, however: a high-backed, upholstered Victorian armchair with a beech and walnut frame **right** mimics French style to suggest its original owner's social status.

THE CHAIR: MASS PRODUCTION

The Model 14 bentwood chair was designed by Michael Thonet in 1859. Unlike Ford's Model T it is still manufactured today by the Gebrüder Thonet company as Model 214 (**opposite left** and in production in Byoritz in the Czech Republic, **below**). The 14/214 became the world's first mass-produced chair and one of the most successful products ever: over 50 million of these chairs have been sold.

The Thonet bentwood chair consists of only six components (plus a few screws and nuts) and the design has remained virtually unchanged for nearly 150 years. It was the first ever flatpack chair, which meant that it could cheaply and easily be shipped around the world.

'Never has anything been created more elegant and better in its conception, more precise in its execution, and more excellently functional,' declared Le Corbusier, who included it in a number of his interiors.

The 14/214 transcends fashion and has had many imitators, not least the Ogla chair by IKEA **opposite right**, a staple of the company's designs for more than 40 years, although it is no longer in production. In its final incarnation, the Ogla was made from recycled plastic and cost less to manufacture and buy than any of the previous models.

Jasper Morrison's Air Chair for Magis (1999) **right** is made as a single unit in gas-injected polypropylene – in its simplicity and everyday quality a modern equivalent to the Thonet bentwood chair.

JAPAN AND THE WEST

The influence of designs and patterns from 'the Orient' dates back to the eighteenth century, from Wedgwood's Willow Pattern tea service to nineteenth-century Paisley textiles. In the late nineteenth century, Japanese culture and products exerted a significant influence on British designers including Christopher Dresser, James Lamb and Philip Webb; and in the USA on the glass and silverware designed by Louis Comfort Tiffany, wallpapers and textiles by Candace Wheeler and furniture by Herter Brothers.

Dresser (1834-1904) in particular was hugely influenced by Japanese products he saw at international exhibitions in London and Paris and on a visit he made to Japan in 1876-7. Above all he admired the focus on function and the simple forms that he saw in Japanese objects, such as this nineteenth-century Japanese Yamanoki ware jar with bluish-white, olive and brown glazes **top right** and vernacular kettle with its minimal surface decoration and simplicity of form **top left**. Dresser set out to embrace these qualities in his own work, such as this electroplated silver coffee pot (1885) **bottom right**. The hemispherical teapot (1880) **bottom left** was manufactured by James Dixon & Son. Made from electroplate with an ebonised wooden handle, it epitomises Dresser's interest in simple, geometric forms. The clever way in which he links the handle to the body at two different points shows how he liked to play with forms but to combine them with function, in this case to avoid the hand coming into contact with the hot metal.

Such was the hunger on the West for things Japanese that products were created specifically for export to Europe and North America. The hand-tinted, coloured photograph, Tea Time in Japan (c. 1900) **opposite above** illustrates the interest in traditional ceremonies as well as the simplicity of Japanese interiors and everyday utensils.

Mary Cassatt's painting, Le Thé or Five o'clock Tea (1880) **opposite below** depicts the importance of tea-drinking to middle-class women. Japanese art was influential on many levels during the late nineteenth century, offering western artists and designers a range of new ideas, from simple form in products, to flat pattern on surfaces, to the idea of the aesthetically minimal but aesthetically integrated interior, to a new approach to pictorial perspective. Together these helped transform modern art and design and to move it away from the impasse of the late Victorian era.

NEW CRAFT

The creative tension between art and industry remains a fertile fulcrum for designers and manufacturers more than 100 years after the death of William Morris.

The German porcelain company Nymphenburg celebrated its 260th anniversary in 2008 by commissioning 16 fashion designers to 'dress' a new edition of its Commedia dell'Arte figurines, originally designed by Franz Anton Bustelli in 1760. Bustelli's work established Nymphenburg's reputation as a world-class manufacturer of porcelain through the delicacy of the figures' poses, their faces, clothes and gestures, and Nymphenburg continues to employ skilled craftspeople to sculpt and paint details by hand. The 'new clothes' – by designers including Victor & Rolf, Vivienne Westwood, Christian Lacroix, Esteban Cortezar and **left** Gareth Pugh – were produced in a limited edition of 25 figures for each designer, reimagining them for the twenty-first century.

The young British designer Russell Pinch runs Pinch Design with his wife from their small house in south London. Pinch's award-winning designs include the Alba console **below right**, its sculptural form inspired by mid-century relief plasterwork. Like its companion piece, the Alba armoire, the interior can be fitted out in a number of combinations or to a client's bespoke specification. The parallels with couture fashion – bespoke or made-to-measure – also provided the creative idea behind the Anders light **above right**, made as a collaboration with one of London's leading milliners. Layers of fabric create an ethereal pendant light, each one of which is unique.

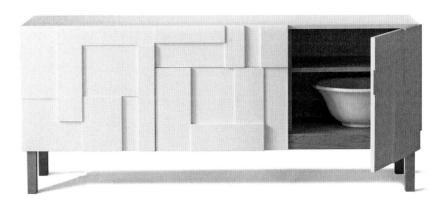

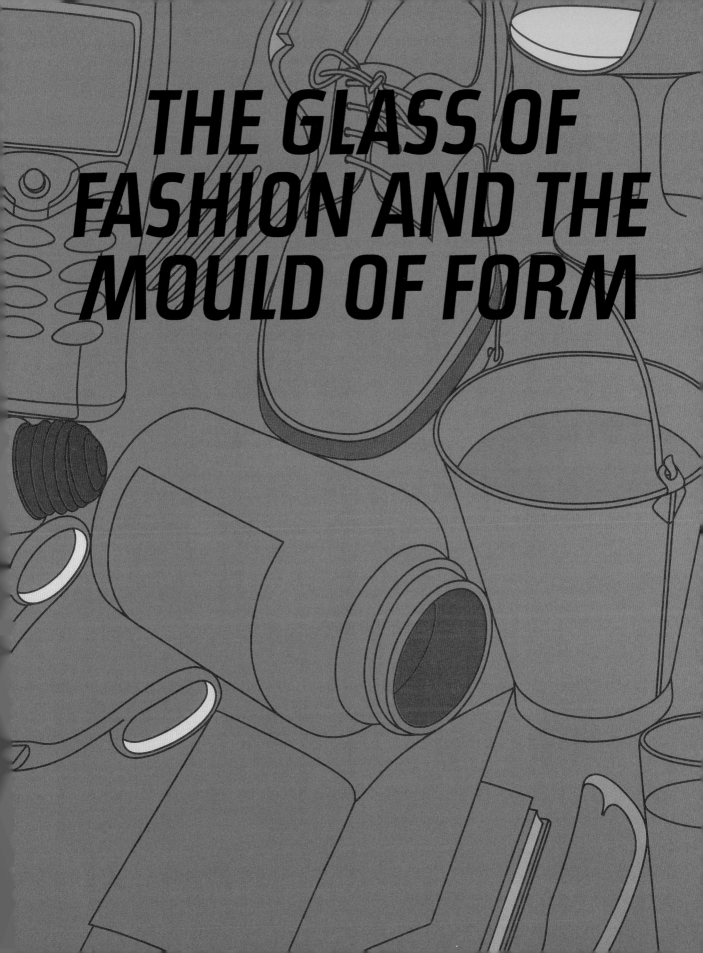

THE GLASS OF FASHION AND THE MOULD OF FORM

DESIGNING THE MODERN HOME

The home is where we have the most direct and most personal relationship with design. Prevailing design fashions may, whether we know it or not, influence our behaviour but we also have control over design by making choices about the things we surround ourselves with. The choices are myriad (Durability and comfort or cutting-edge style? Familiarity or novelty? Deep red wallpaper or white paint?) but also fraught, because we recognise that our personal identities are most dramatically formed and expressed in our homes. Many of us judge others by their design choices – by the way their homes look, whether they have 'taste' or 'class' – and we know we will be so judged.

For all but the very wealthy, design has not always played such an important role in the home. But by the middle of the nineteenth century, industrialisation had given large numbers of people easy access to mass-produced tables, chairs, knives and forks, soup tureens, candlesticks, flower vases, picture frames, carpets, furnishing textiles, sewing machines, and a host of other goods. Once inside the home these goods were arranged and displayed by the housewife who was able, in the process, to make her own choices and become a designer herself. The Victorian 'Cult of Domesticity' emphasised the importance of values (in this case, family values) being embedded into the actual material stuff that people surrounded themselves with in their domestic settings, and from then on architects and designers also focused on the home as a place where they could influence people's private lives and identities and directly shape their lifestyles.

The first three decades of the twentieth century were the period of the architectural and design modern movement, also called 'modernism'. Modernists sought to move away from Victorian bourgeois materialism and to use the underlying principles of mass production – standardisation etc. – to create a new architecture. They aligned themselves with the ideas outlined in 1907 by the Viennese architect, Adolf Loos, in his famous book *Ornament and Crime* that aligned decoration with the work of primitive cultures and its rejection with advanced ones. Modernism came to be characterised by its simple, functional, undecorated buildings and objects created following the principles of 'form follows function' and 'truth to materials'. During this time home was where modernist architects and designers – fired by visions of a new, democratic future, and of a rational way of life unencumbered by material possessions – saw the greatest opportunity for real change.

The story of design in the home has a number of threads. A radical, progressive strand viewed the entire house, architecture and interior, holistically. From Charles Rennie Mackintosh and Frank Lloyd Wright to the members of the De Stijl group and those of the Bauhaus to Le Corbusier, the home became a total work of art, whether, for example, expressed in the flowing, symbolic lines of Art Nouveau (or the more linear ones of Northern European Jugendstil) or the clutter-free, clean and clinical spaces proposed

Michael Craig-Martin's *Wallpaper Painting (Blue)* from 2004 **previous pages** creates a repeat motif of everyday designed objects – light bulbs, buckets, a Nokia phone, a Saarinen chair – that fill our domestic spaces and help us to define our sense of who we are.

Publications telling people how to decorate their homes, and what is or is not 'good taste' or 'good design', proliferated in the early twentieth century and continue to play an important role in our lives today **opposite**. The interior decorator Elsie de Wolfe's 1913 book *The House in Good Taste* **top left** depicted the homes she had created for herself and others, while Herbert Bayer's *Bauhaus* publication **top right** was a manifesto for the ideas of that radical 1920s design educational institution. Herbert Read's *Art and Industry* (1934) **bottom left** tackled the aesthetics of industrial mass production and 'the capacity of the machine to produce works of art.' American designer Todd Oldham's *Camp Nest* monograph (2008) **bottom right** about the countryside artistic retreat of Joe Holtzman, the editor of (the now defunct) *Nest* magazine expresses the ideas of a much more recent taste élite.

by the modernists. The last group also looked to modern scientific principles from factory-based time-and-motion studies to determine how interior spaces could be best used, producing the 'rational' home and the fitted kitchen. A third strand focussed on the design of status-affirming consumer durables. These were produced by American industrial designers of the inter-war years – who were equally active in their creation of streamlined office equipment, factory machines and passenger trains – and filled the market-led conception of the 'dream home'. There was also a more particular, often feminine design ideal which saw decisions about home design as expressing the individual personality of the home owner. This ideal was ultimately successful, although it arose from women's ultimately unsuccessful ambition, in the first half of the twentieth century, to drive the profession of interior decoration.

Femininity in the home

By the end of the nineteenth century, the home was very firmly established as the woman's sphere of influence, and the look of the interior, its contents and the way they were arranged, were her responsibility. Industrialisation had moved most paid work out of the house and marked the beginning of the close association between women and domesticity that has characterised the modern home. In her 1913 book, *The House in Good Taste,* the American pioneer interior decorator, Elsie de Wolfe, went as far as to claim, that, 'It is the personality of the mistress that the home expresses. Men are forever guests in our homes, no matter how much happiness they may find there.'

The link between women and the home had, and continues to have, a significant effect on domestic design. Indeed in the middle years of the nineteenth century woman's role as the key consumer of fashionable artefacts for the home caused many design reformers to hold her personally responsible for the debasement of aesthetic values that they saw all around them. 'In the eyes of Materfamilias', proclaimed Charles Eastlake in his 1868 advice book, *Hints on Household Taste* for example, 'there is no upholstery which could possibly surpass that which the most fashionable upholsterer supplied ... When did people first adopt the monstrous notion that the "last pattern out" must be the best?' The modern movement architects and designers built on that critique and their involvement in the home derived largely from their desire to rescue it from bourgeois materialism and feminine taste.

However, in the 1870s and 1880s a number of (male) architects and designers, linked to what was called the aesthetic movement, celebrated the link between femininity and the home and embraced the idea that the domestic interior should be seen, like dress, as a marker of fashion awareness, or 'taste'. Artist-designers like Aubrey Beardsley and literary figures such as Oscar Wilde embraced Aestheticism, with its credo of pure beauty in art and design –'art for art's sake'– and in the home, aesthete architects and designers E.W. Godwin, Bruce Talbert and Thomas Jeckyll argued for a harmonised, unifying interior. They wanted to replace heavy Victorian designs and bright hues with lighter, fresher, Japanese-inspired shapes and more muted colours, bringing in the natural forms of sunflowers and lilies and a range of Oriental items, from Japanese fans to blue-and-white pottery. The aesthetic interior was made accessible to the new middle classes through advice books on home decoration written by authors such as Eastlake and Mrs. Haweis. With their help uneducated housewives were

Aubrey Beardsley's illustration from the 1894 edition of Oscar Wilde's *Salome* contains numerous references to peacocks, the symbol *par excellence* of the artists, designers and architects associated with the aesthetic movement, a hugely popular phenomenon in Britain and the US through the 1870s and 1880s. Along with Japanese fans and ceramic objects, lilies and sunflowers, the natural but highly decorative form of the peacock exemplified a pure beauty – 'art for art's for sake' – that characterised aestheticism. This commitment to beauty could be found in the highly decorated homes of the artistic élite, as well as other more humble dwellings influenced by the home decorating manuals of the day.

able to become interior designers and create fashionable, artistic interiors in their own homes.

Design and detail

Around the turn of the century several progressive architects and designers also became preoccupied with the domestic interior as it began to take on more and more cultural significance. In Scotland the Glaswegian architect Charles Rennie Mackintosh, sometimes working with his wife, the artist and designer Margaret Macdonald, created a number of innovative domestic interiors both in buildings he designed and in others he simply refurbished. He pioneered the 'total design' of house and interior: strong lines and graceful, symbolic forms in the architecture, rooms, chairs, textiles, stained glass and metalwork all combined to make an organic, harmonious whole. In the Hill House, a building and interior that Mackintosh designed himself, and which was constructed in Helensburgh between 1902 and 1904 for the publisher Walter Blackie, a strong, solid exterior contains remarkably spacious, light-filled rooms. Mackintosh's built-in furniture and his typically careful use of colour and repeated motifs created an exceptional sense of harmony between the inside and the outside of the house.

Mackintosh is often associated stylistically with a movement in architecture and the decorative arts that swept across Southern Europe and the US at the turn of the century. The fashionable but short-lived Art Nouveau, whose flowing, sinuous lines and organic forms were inspired by nature, and Jugendstil, its more restrained Northern European geometric equivalent, also embraced a holistic view of design, and its architects and designers worked to maintain visual consistency both inside and outside their buildings.

A number of other European architects and designers shared the radically new ideas about integrated domestic design that Mackintosh developed in Scotland, among them the Belgian Henry van de Velde, the German Peter Behrens, and the Austrian Josef Hoffmann. Influenced by Art Nouveau and Jugendstil, many had been associated with the Deutscher Werkbund (pages 51–2), and all were committed to the idea of the *Gesamtkunstwerk* – roughly translated as 'total work of art'– which gave architects considerable

The library at Charles Rennie Mackintosh's Glasgow School of Art (built 1897–1909) **left** is a true *Gesamtkunstwerk* (total work of art). The visual coherence of pillars, light fixtures and items of furniture is indicative of Mackintosh's approach to interior design, one that he applied to domestic spaces as well as public buildings – from churches to tea rooms.

The Wiener Werkstätte (Vienna Workshops, 1903–1932) represented the work of architects and designers – Josef Hoffmann, J.M. Olbrich, and Koloman Moser, among others – who promoted a new approach towards domestic decoration that linked surface pattern with structure in an innovative way. The emergent aesthetic embraced architecture, furniture, ceramic, glass and metal decorative objects, textiles and graphic design **above** and became highly fashionable, spreading across the Atlantic in the years following the First World War.

control over the spaces within their buildings. Both van de Velde and Behrens took this approach to its limit in the homes they created for themselves and their families. 'Bloemenwerf', van de Velde's house in the Brussels suburb of Uccle, was conceived as a whole, inside and out, even down to the dress that the architect created for his wife. Behrens, like Mackintosh, introduced repeated motifs and built-in furniture into the furnishings of his family house in Darmstadt as a means of unifying and linking the interior with the architecture that housed it.

In the US, the architect Frank Lloyd Wright was evolving similar ideas in his development of an American domestic ideal based on what came to be called the 'Prairie House', the American equivalent of the vernacular-inspired Arts & Crafts home. As an antidote to what Wright considered to be the cramped and boxed-in nature of the Victorian house, his more geometric designs used expansive horizontal lines and, radically, the interiors were open-plan. He built a number of examples in Oak Park, a suburb of Chicago, including a house for himself and his family which contained a studio for him to work in. He used the house as a test-bed for many of his fundamentally new ideas about interior domestic space, including domed ceilings to create a greater sense of space. Like Mackintosh, he wanted aesthetic unity inside and out, designing built-in furniture as well as chairs, tables, lamps, stained-glass windows and textiles to furnish his buildings.

As van de Velde had done, Wright also designed clothing for his wife so that she would blend in with his interior aesthetic. Innovative dress, inspired by the dress reform movement that sought to free women from the constraints of the corset, also played a key role within the work of another highly influential design group, the Wiener Werkstätte (Vienna Workshops), who

designed and created fabrics, furniture, lamps, jewellery and ceramics using simple forms, restrained decoration and geometric patterning. Their adherence to the total work of art ideal is displayed in buildings such as the Stoclet Palace, a private house in Brussels, designed by Josef Hoffman, and filled with Werkstätte furnishings and decorative objects. Hoffmann also created an interior for a store owned by the Viennese dress designers, the Flöge sisters, who were involved with the dress reform movement and who used Werkstätte-designed textiles for their clothes. The relationship of dress to architecture and to other design disciplines was to become a recurrent theme within the European modern movement of the inter-war years.

The Russian choreographer Sergei Diaghilev's Ballets Russes company toured Europe in the years leading up to the First World War. The spectacular, brightly coloured and decorated costumes worn by its dancers **above** and used in stage sets proved hugely influential. The French couturier Paul Poiret, who extended his interest in fashion to the interior with the formation of his Atelier Martine, was especially drawn to the ballet and transformed his designs as a result of his exposure to it.

The Russian Constructivist movement of the early post-revolutionary years embraced a new abstract aesthetic and applied it to fine art, architecture and design, including fashion and graphic design. Liubov Popova's illustration for a woman's coat (1924) **left** combines strict geometry with abstract surface pattern and imagines a completely new direction for fashionable dress.

Frank Lloyd Wright's Ennis House in Los Feliz, California (1924) **right** is an innovative design using 'textile blocks' – pre-cast concrete blocks with decoratively patterned surfaces. Wright liked to design all the details of a house, both structural and decorative, such as this stained-glass window, to ensure the artistic unity of his vision.

COCO CHANEL

Gabrielle 'Coco' Chanel (1883–1971) above was one of France's leading couturiers. She embraced a modern image of twentieth-century women, and created simple and elegant clothes for them, many of them inspired by menswear. 'I gave women a sense of freedom; I gave them back their bodies: bodies that were drenched in sweat, due to fashion's finery, lace, corsets, underclothes, padding,' she said, and thought women should lead modern, independent lives.

Chanel was born in a poorhouse but rose to fame as a fashion designer, financing her business in part through love affairs with Etienne Balsan, a French race-horse breeder, and the English polo player, Edward 'Boy' Capel. Starting out with hats, Chanel moved on to women's sportswear and finally on to general clothing such as the suit and blouse **above right** photographed by Horst P. Horst in 1938. Her progressive views on women's empowerment did not extend to other political beliefs. Where many modernist architects and designers associated their practice with broadly socialist principles and fled continental Europe for Britain and the USA in the 1930s, Chanel spent the Second World War in a suite at the Ritz Hotel in Paris, protected by her Nazi lover.

The iconic Chanel jacket, largely unchanged from season to season, ditched complex and constraining tailoring for lightweight materials and machine sewing: the trademark heavy buttons and curbed chain trims help to give the jacket weight. 'Simplicity is the keynote of all true elegance,' she told *Harper's Bazaar* in 1923.

In 1921, she created Chanel No. 5 – the first perfume to have a designer's name attached to it **right**. Its name supposedly arose from Chanel's asking the perfumier, Ernest Beaux, to create six fragrances for her to choose, numbered 1 to 6, 5 being her favourite. It has been on sale ever since; estimates are that a bottle of No. 5 is sold worldwide every 55 seconds.

Asked in 1953 what she wore in bed, Marilyn Monroe (photographed by Michael Ochs in 1955 **right**) famously answered, 'Why, Chanel No. 5, of course.' Chanel herself declared that, 'a woman should wear fragrance wherever she expects to be kissed.' The perfume is another modern icon. The bottle has been silk-screened by Andy Warhol; the packaging is in the collection of the Museum of Modern Art in New York; and the scent was the subject of a multi-million dollar commercial directed by Baz Luhrmann and starring Nicole Kidman – signs of its enduring significance.

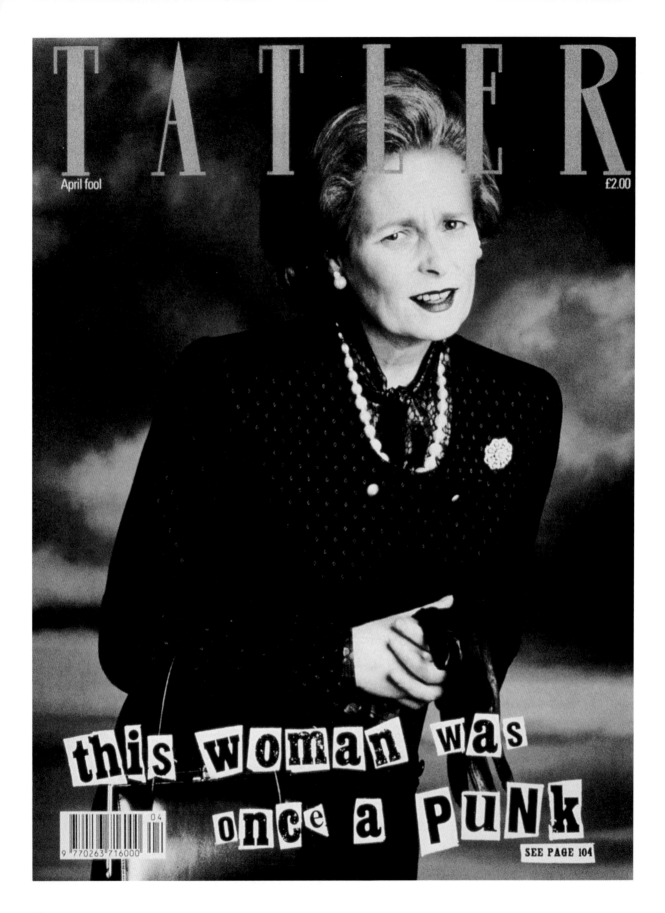

I'M NOT TRYING TO DO SOMETHING DIFFERENT, I'M TRYING TO DO THE SAME THING BUT IN A DIFFERENT WAY. – VIVIENNE WESTWOOD

Coco Chanel was a revolutionary in the male-dominated world of Paris couture – a woman who designed clothes for women, rather than for men to objectify.

Foremost among today's female fashion designers, Vivienne Westwood has always associated her designs with the political. 'There is always a polemic in my clothes,' she has said. In 1989, she appeared on the cover of Tatler **left** explaining, 'Margaret Thatcher has always been one of the world's best-dressed people. Her politics were appalling, but her look gave her incredible presence.'

Like Chanel, Jean Muir, photographed in 1966, **top left** created simple, easy-to-wear fashions, a discipline that has kept the Anne Klein label, founded by Klein and continued (until 1989) by Donna Karan, successful for more than 40 years, and epitomised by the Spring 2008 catwalk collection **below left**.

Prada became an international fashion force when founder Mario Prada's granddaughter Miuccia inherited the company in 1978. (Ironically, Mario believed that women had no head for business.) Miuccia Prada calls her designs 'uniforms', created for modern, working women. Like Chanel, she had created liberating women's sportswear, advertised here in 1999 **above**.

The feminine touch

At the same time as Wright was exerting male control over the design of the home in the US, however, this masculine, architecture-led model of domestic design was being challenged, in the same country, by a group of 'lady decorators' who set out to design the home along more overtly feminine lines. By the 1890s and early 1900s a number of artistically able women – Candace Wheeler and Elsie de Wolfe among them – had begun to realise that women could use the expertise they acquired furnishing their own homes to make a living for themselves as professional interior decorators. Wheeler worked with Louis Comfort Tiffany's decorating company for a few years before branching out on her own. De Wolfe, a successful Broadway actress in the 1890s and well known for the couture dresses, designed by Worth, Doucet and others, that she had worn on stage, moved seamlessly from amateur to professional status. Her personal design philosophy was rooted in what were seen at the time as feminine features of the interior, i.e. domesticity, comfort, decoration and an emphasis on personal expression. She was less interested in the architectural shell of the house than in the expressive potential of the arrangements of the furniture, furnishings and decorative details of the domestic interior which, for her, were an extension of dress. She stressed the importance of historical styles – especially those of eighteenth-century France – while simultaneously giving them a modern, fashionable twist in order to appeal to her early-twentieth-century, nouveau-riche, fashion- and status-conscious clientèle. Most importantly de Wolfe emphasised that the thoughtfully decorated home could convey the identity of the modern women. It was a hugely successful formula which quickly made her rich and famous. A number of other women were quick to follow in her footsteps, among them Dorothy Draper and Ruby Ross Wood in the US and Syrie Maugham in England. While they were hugely influential up to the 1930s, they were largely superseded by men (who had always held sway in mainland Europe) in the post-war years, at the same time that the term 'interior decorator' fell from favour and was replaced by the more modern 'interior designer'.

The rational home

Two other main areas of activity influenced the design of the modern home in the years after 1900. Firstly the domestic economy movement, also referred to in the early twentieth century as 'household engineering' or 'scientific management in the home', and, secondly, the architectural and design modern movement that, borrowing from scientific management, proposed a completely new model for the home and its furnishings.

The first signs of the application to the home of the rational ideas developed in the factory were visible in the US in the middle years of the nineteenth century. Catherine Beecher had 'first made the art of housekeeping a scientific study' in her 1869 publication *The American Woman's Home*. Her aim had been to give Christian women pride and satisfaction in the creation of an efficient home and, to that end, she had proposed the idea of the 'rational kitchen', which, at that time, she situated at the heart of the house with a large table at its centre.

However, the rational household movement's greatest influence on the design of the home came through Christine Frederick's *The New Housekeeping* of 1913, which had been published earlier in instalments in the *Ladies' Home Journal* (of which Frederick was the household editor). Frederick was familiar with the tenets of Taylorism, the ideas, that is, of Frederick Winslow Taylor,

who had pioneered time-and-motion studies in factories and advocated the rationalisation of tasks so that they could be undertaken more quickly and efficiently. His work involved arranging tools for effective use and reducing the number of steps taken by workers in the performance of their tasks. Later in the century time-and-motion studies were joined by anthropometrics – the study of human measurements – and ergonomics – the study of how men and machines connect. Over the years the impact of these studies has been enormous on a wide range of products and

spaces, from office chairs to the driving seats of cars and the cockpits of aeroplanes.

Frederick took Taylor's ideas directly into the home, focusing on the kitchen and laundry as the rooms in which most productive labour took place. She set out to apply the principle of 'step-saving' to the domestic sphere with great enthusiasm. Explaining that, 'I won't have you men doing all the great and noble things! I'm going to find out how these experts conduct investigations, and all about it, and then apply it to my factory, my business, my home', she focused on the idea of step-saving in the kitchen and

Kitchen design in the 1920s was strongly influenced by kitchens in trains and ships' galleys. The space-saving efficiency that was necessary in these confined spaces was widely emulated in designs for the home. The modern iconography and graphic style of this poster **left** promoting the use of the restaurant bar of a train is typical of the great French typographer and designer, Adolphe Mouron Cassandre, whose other work includes iconic posters for the Normandie liner and Dubonnet, as well as the YSL logo for Yves Saint Laurent.

Hard at work in her highly efficient kitchen, this overall-clad housewife from 1937 is ensuring that her kitchen floor is clean **above**. Aesthetically this space has little to link it with the comfortable domesticity that is undoubtedly on offer in the living-room. Instead its white surfaces and materials evoke a rational, laboratory-like workspace.

produced a number of diagrams depicting good kitchen planning. In her well-organised spaces the numbers of steps needed to perform the tasks of preparing, cooking and cleaning up after a meal were reduced to a minimum. Following the example of men's clubs, because it side-stepped issues about feminine domesticity, she positioned the kitchen as a small room at the rear of the house, creating what resembled a small, but efficient, domestic 'laboratory' in which the housewife – clad like a scientist in a white overall, and seated on a high stool from which she could reach everything she needed – was destined to spend most of her time.

Although Frederick took her approach from factory planning, her proposal that tools needed to be grouped together for specific tasks suggested a craft, rather than a divided labour, process. Indeed she saw the housewife as both a manager and a worker. Above all Frederick's ideas about the home confirmed a shift away from its Victorian associations with moral, spiritual, and aesthetic values. Her work had a huge influence on subsequent ideas about domestic space planning and it encouraged a break with the backward-looking Victorian ideology of the home in which function was subservient to form.

While Frederick didn't address the issue of design directly, she established an important framework for a subsequent re-design of the domestic kitchen that was to have far-reaching effects. Translations of her book into German and French informed the European modernist architects who were beginning, in the 1920s, to rethink the design of the home, in particular the kitchen, along the lines of examples outside the home, such as Pullman dining cars. Their reasons for drawing on such models were based on their desire to rid the home of Victorian bourgeois domesticity and to align it with the democratic, rational values that, they believed, characterised life in the modern world.

The fitted kitchen

The desire to design the kitchen along the rational lines proposed by the advocates of 'scientific management' was a recurrent modernist theme through the 1920s and the 1930s. In 1927, Erna Meyer (Germany's Christine Frederick) collaborated with the Dutch architect, J. J. P. Oud, on a kitchen for the Weissenhof exhibition in Stuttgart which featured the, by now familiar, open shelving and housewife's stool and workbench that had been proposed by Frederick back in 1913. The architect Ernst May, who was involved in the redevelopment of Frankfurt, saw the Meyer/Oud kitchen in Stuttgart, and, as a direct result, commissioned a thorough programme of research on the standardised kitchen he was developing for the Frankfurt scheme. The research involved delving into psychology and the application of scientific management. In a radical way, design was now to be used to affect behaviour – here, to make housewives more efficient and more satisfied.

As part of his research May brought in the architect, Margarete Schütte-Lihotzky from Vienna. She set about designing what came to known as the 'Frankfurt kitchen', one of the most influential examples of rational kitchen planning. She took inspiration from kitchens outside the home – the ship's galley, the kitchen in the railway dining car and the lunch wagon in particular – that had been created to serve food to large numbers of people in as efficient a way as possible. Like her predecessors she stressed the importance of step-saving and efficient storage and developed what has been described as 'a work station where all implements were a simple extension of the operator's hand'.

Margarete Schütte-Lihotzky (1897–2000, photographed in 1927, **left**) was one of the few female architects to play a part in the international modern movement. Trained in Vienna she was brought to Germany by the architect Ernst May and her original thinking about kitchen design earned her a lasting reputation.

Her Frankfurt kitchen (1926) **opposite** was designed for Ernst May as part of his work for the Municipal Housing Department in Frankfurt, a standardised kitchen that was installed in 10,000 flats and the prototype for all fitted kitchens since then. Building on the ideas of Christine Frederick's book, *Household Engineering* (1913), the Frankfurt kitchen went one step further, combining efficiency with good looks in a small space (1.9 x 3.4m); the housewife could undertake all her tasks using the minimum number of steps. 'The problem of rationalising the housewife's work is equally important to all classes of society. Both the middle-class women, who often work without any help [servants] in their homes, and also the women of the worker class, who often have to work in other jobs, are overworked to the point that their stress is bound to have serious consequences for public health at large,' she wrote in 1926.

THE BAUHAUS

The German Bauhaus, which opened in Weimar in 1919 and transferred to Dessau in 1925, was a radical design educational institution, the model for today's art schools in many ways. It taught its students to work directly with materials and to follow the principle of 'form follows function'. The Dessau buildings **above** were designed by the school's first director, Walter Gropius, and provided an appropriately modern setting for this educational experiment.

The Dessau buildings included offices and homes for key members of staff executed in the same modern idiom as its main buildings. Objects designed at the school, such as the tubular steel and canvas chair by Marcel Breuer, were used to furnish the interiors, including the director's office **above right**.

The Bauhaus curriculum **below right** began with a six-month elementary course, shown at the outside ring of the circle. A further three years were spent studying nature, materials, construction theory and practice under the tuition of two masters, one an artist and the other a craftsman, who included in their number Paul Klee, Wassily Kandinsky, Oskar Schlemmer, the painter and mystic Johannes Itten, László Moholy-Nagy and Josef Albers. Students finally devoted their time to one of a number of workshops, some of them shown as the inner circle: wood, metal, textiles, colour, glass, clay and stone. The relatively few female students who were recruited gravitated to the textiles workshop.

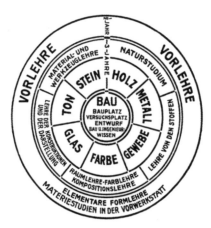

Photography was not taught at the Bauhaus until 1929, although the Constructivist artist, László Moholy-Nagy, began experimenting with form and techniques when he arrived at the school in 1923 to lead the preliminary course and the metal workshop. Unencumbered by the formal structures of coursework, photography became a sort of play. One student in particular, Lux Feininger – son of the one of the masters, the painter, Lyonel Feininger – was seldom without his camera. The shot of students playing football (c. 1928) **right** is typical of his exuberant style.

THE BAUHAUS WAS THE BEGINNING OF THE ART SCHOOL AS AN ALTERNATIVE WAY OF LIFE. – FIONA MACCARTHY

The rigorous strictures of modernism and the fashions of time mean that the Bauhaus is as beloved by architects and academics as it is perhaps misconceived by the general public. Efficiently managed archives and learned monographs have enshrined the Bauhaus within a particularly esoteric framework.

In fact, by many accounts, life at the Bauhaus was liberating and inspiring: traditional disciplines melded and experimentation was encouraged. 'Fancy dress' – albeit inspired by theory – was widely practised, not only in the famous Triadic Ballet costumes by Oscar Schlemmer but in a number of balls, including one in 1922 in Berlin attended by the Dutch painter and theorist Theo van Doesburg **right**. To its critics at the time, the Bauhaus was as morally degenerate as Weimar Berlin, famously depicted in some of the novels of Christopher Ishwerwood and in the 1966 musical (and subsequent 1972 movie), *Cabaret*. Like Kurt Weill and Bertolt Brecht, the choreographer Kurt Jooss and composer Fritz Cohen championed avant-garde performance, their most famous work being The Green Table (1932, seen in a revival by the American Ballet Company in 2007, **above**) which was performed just a year before Adolf Hitler became Chancellor of Germany and Jooss fled to Holland and then England.

One of the most prodigious and brilliant champions of performance art was the Australian-born Leigh Bowery (1961–94) **left**, who dominated the polysexual art/club scene of London in the 1980s and early '90s as well as being a muse for the painter Lucien Freud. His work, including collaborations with the dancer-choreographer Michael Clark and the band The Fall, challenged ideas of form and identity. 'If clothes are going to mean anything they've got to threaten or challenge,' he said. 'If they have that edge they should provoke people into thinking.'

Schütte-Lihotzky attached a continuous work surface to the wall, and fitted a wooden plate holder below the glazed wall cupboards. Unlike the rather basic kitchens depicted by Frederick, her kitchen was visually integrated, elegant and overtly modern. Although the deep blue that she chose to use was supposedly effective in repelling flies it also added considerably to the kitchen's visual impact. Above all, the materials – linoleum, glass and steel among them – gave the room a sophisticated, modern look. Most significantly the kitchen, which was designed for Frankfurt's new public housing, went immediately into mass production.

Lines of living and the geometry of design

The work of Frederick and Schütte-Lihotzky offered a practical example of the way in which modern design could determine and not merely reflect the way people lived, and was important as modernist architects, artists and designers went on to develop an aesthetic for the modern home. Those active in the Netherlands in the years around the First World War, and associated with the movement called de Stijl, were particularly innovative and influential. The worlds of art, design and architecture were closely linked to each other in their eyes but no longer associated with the concept of taste. Rather the de Stijl designers proposed that function should drive everything, and that the basic, abstract language of art – form, surface and colour – should be used to communicate function. A number of highly radical designs emerged as a result, especially from the hands of the cabinet-maker Gerrit Rietveld. His design for a house in Utrecht for a widow, Truus Schröder, for example, followed the success of his famous, starkly geometric Red/ Blue Chair of 1917. In designing the chair Rietveld had started out with the idea of creating a 'sitting

object' made up of a series of planes and their intersections. He let the planes overlap with each other in order to emphasise their intersections, and he used colour – red, blue, yellow, black and white – to identify the different planes. Ultimately, in line with other modernist designs, his chair was a study of the construction of a chair rather than a comfortable sitting-object.

In his 1924 foray into domestic architecture Rietveld approached the task as a cabinet-maker, adopting an 'inside out' approach. The first floor was the most radically conceived space in the house. It could be either left as a fluid, open space, or else sliding and revolving panels could create a number of discrete spaces – individual bedrooms for the family members among them. Each room had a balcony that served to bring the outside in and to take the inside out. At one corner the windows opened outwards at ninety degrees with the effect that, as she sat at her desk, Mrs. Schröder was completely exposed to the outside world, an experience that contrasted dramatically with inhabiting a Victorian home where the outside had been completely shut out.

The design of the Schröder house suggested a particular idea of the modern family – one that had flexible living arrangements and wanted to live an active and engaged intellectual life without being encumbered by too many possessions. The spaces inside the house were as adaptable as they could be and the functions within them were defined by colour. Rietveld achieved maximum efficiency and flexibility in the upper floor of the house by using Japanese-style sliding doors and by storing furnishing items when not in use. Folding tables cantilevered out from walls and flaps of wood covered the ventilation slits in the window frames. Above all Rietveld sought to create a harmonious environment, defined by colour, light and space.

The house that the Dutch architect-designer, Gerrit Rietveld, created for the widow, Truus Schröder in 1924 **opposite** transposed the ideas of the artists of the Dutch de Stijl group – Piet Mondrian and Theo van Doesburg among them – into a domestic interior. The effects were utterly radical and transforming. The ground floor hallway with the stairs leading to the dramatic, open-plan first floor revealed how Rietveld integrated built-in furniture – the little bench on the landing – with the architectural frame. The striking use of horizontals and verticals reflects de Stijl paintings.

Perhaps Rietveld's most famous design was his Red/Blue chair (1917) **left** which was an exercise in geometry and in the use of colour to define plane and surface. Although it resembles a 'sitting object' it is a work exploring spatial manipulation at heart and was not meant to make a comfortable seat. Originally, the chair was painted in black, grey and white; Rietveld changed the colours a year later after meeting the Dutch painter, Piet Mondrian, in 1918. The Red/Blue chair remains one of the most controversial objects of the architectural and design modern movement.

Form, form, form

The ideas of the rational house and scientific management of domestic spaces directly informed the design of an experimental house, the Haus am Horn, that was created in 1923 by staff and students of the German Bauhaus, a design school set up in 1919 by the architect Walter Gropius, first in Weimar, and, from 1923, in Dessau (pages 80–81). Influenced also by de Stijl, the house included a number of novel features, including the use of colour to denote different interior spaces, as well as built-in furniture, both following Rietveld. The kitchen, designed by Benita Otte and Ernst Gebhardt, was especially interesting. In line with Christine Frederick's recommendations it contained a workbench and a stool on which the housewife could perch while she performed her tasks. It went further, however, adding eye-level cupboards with doors on them so as to avoid any contamination of their contents by dust. One of the kitchen's most innovative features was the inclusion of a set of standardised, labelled ceramic containers, designed by Theodor Bogler, the precursors of the containers labelled 'sugar', 'raisins' or 'flour' that feature in so many contemporary kitchens.

The Haus am Horn was just one of the many designs made at the Bauhaus that went on to influence the appearance of the modern domestic interior for many years to come in both Europe and North America. The Bauhaus was, first and foremost, an experiment in design education which encouraged its students to work with abstract form, applied to a range of materials – wood, ceramics, metal and textiles – in the creation of functional products that were primarily destined for the home, from chairs to teapots to lamps to rugs. The objects created in the Bauhaus workshops were conceived as prototypes for factory production, although,

while a few tentative links with industry were forged in the 1920s, its most memorable objects generally went into production outside Germany after the school was closed by the Nazis in 1933.

As well as revolutionizing design education the Bauhaus also contributed to the development of modern design in a number of important ways. It not only pushed boundaries forward in the areas of ceramics and weaving it also influenced modern graphic design and typography. When the Hungarian, László Moholy-Nagy was appointed in 1923 he introduced to the Bauhaus the principles of what came to be called the 'New Typography', an approach to graphic design that had previously been developed by others, including El Lissitsky in Russia. This focused on clarity of communication and prioritised the use of geometric and unadorned sans-serif type and asymmetry. Herbert Bayer led the Bauhaus typography workshop, working there with his Universal type. Later, after he had set up home in the USA, Bayer became one of the twentieth century's most influential graphic designers.

Most importantly a new vision of the home was developed at the Bauhaus that focused on space rather than mass, and which required domestic objects to blend seamlessly with the architecture that contained them. Marcel Breuer's famous 'Wassily' chair (page 102), for example, was a reworking of the traditional leather armchair found in men's clubs. His use of tubular steel (inspired by his bicycle) enabled him to develop a skeletal version of that conventional object without sacrificing any of its comfort. Emphasising structure rather than volume, and using leather strips as supports for the body, Breuer's radical vision was of a comfortable and visually pleasing sitting-object that had significant presence without disturbing the architectural space it occupied.

While there were Dutch precedents for Breuer's work – the designs of Rietveld and Mart Stam, for instance – Breuer's designs are the ones that have lasted and, in the early twenty-first century, they continue to grace spare modernist interiors. Other lasting pieces from the Bauhaus include Wilhelm Wagenfeld's metal and glass table lamp and Marianne Brandt's little metal teapot. These radical reformulations of existing objects were made possible by their designers' deep questioning of the ways in which these objects performed their functions and exploited their materials. None of them were uniquely intended for the home – indeed their inspirations, and their materials came from the public arena for the most part, but they succeeded, nonetheless, in creating a radically new aesthetic for the modern home and its contents. Importantly, their ultimate aim was not aesthetically focused, however. Rather, they set out to change behaviour and to realise a vision of modern living.

Adventures in space

The new 'machine style' home was enthusiastically received in other European countries (though less so in the more traditionally-minded Britain). In France a number of progressive architects, Le Corbusier and Robert Mallet-Stevens among them, created stunning examples for their most adventurous clients. Le Corbusier's Villa Savoye, located in Poissy on the outskirts of Paris, was a dramatic, flat-roofed, white house raised from the ground on concrete 'pilotis' (stilts). Built between 1928 and 1931 the Villa Savoye was an exercise in space, light, texture and colour. It was dominated by what Le Corbusier called the 'architectural promenade', the systematic routes that took people through the house. Whether on the gentle ramp, or on the spiral staircase that wound itself through the three floors of the building and up on

to the roof terrace, it left one in no doubt about the presence of the controlling hand of the architect in his creation. At any point on the promenade the view was carefully staged. Le Corbusier also exploited the possibilities of new materials and built-in furniture wherever possible. Tables cantilevered out of walls, and sliding glass doors were fitted to the kitchen cupboards. The client, Madame Savoye, ultimately found the elegant 'machine' rather too dehumanised to spend much time in, however.

Designers in a number of different countries took up the Bauhaus baton in the 1930s, creating objects for the home that focused on function and materials and that displayed a minimal, geometric aesthetic. Walter Gropius and Marcel Breuer both spent time in Britain during their exile from Nazi Germany, both of them on their way to permanent residence in the US.

Jack Pritchard's company Isokon was one of the most forward-thinking British furniture-makers of the 1930s. Pritchard supported designers fleeing Nazi Germany, among them Egon Riss, who did odd jobs for Pritchard in return for accommodation, among them the Donkey bookcase (1939) **left**. Allen Lane, publisher of Penguin paperbacks, took a shine to the design and inserted 100,000 promotional leaflets into the back of his books, and the design was renamed the Penguin Donkey. Success was thwarted by the outbreak of war, and only about 100 originals were made, although reproductions are still manufactured today. Isokon commissioned Donkey 2 from Ernest Race in 1963 and Donkey 3 from Shin and Tomoko Azumi in 2003.

The Canadian design duo Fishbol Atelier's recent Bookseat (2008) **above** is eerily reminiscent of Riss's earlier design, although it exudes a post-modern playfulness. Combining two functions in one – bookcase and chair – it wittily exploits the need for multifunctional designs as contemporary urban homes become smaller.

LE CORBUSIER

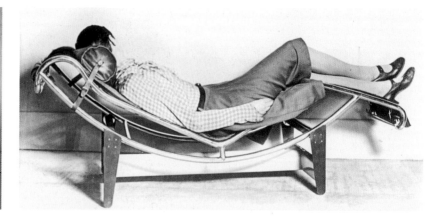

Of all the modern movement architects and designers to apply their skills to domestic architecture, the Swiss-born Charles-Edouard Jeanneret-Gris (1887–1925) – Le Corbusier – was probably the most influential and articulate about his ideas. He famously declared that 'the house is a machine for living in', and adopted the pseudonym Le Corbusier in the early 1920s. He is pictured **above** in the 1940s beside a model for his Unité d'Habitation in Marseilles.

The Villa Savoye (1928–31) **middle right** realised many of Le Corbusier's early ideas about domestic architecture, with its 'pilotis' (stilts), ribbon windows, open spaces and inside/outside ambiguities. However, its owner, Madame Savoye, found it perhaps too machine-like to live in for extended periods.

At the same time, Le Corbusier collaborated with Charlotte Perriand and his cousin Pierre Jeanneret on their frequently copied chaise-longue (1928) **top right** on which Perriand lies with her eyes averted and wearing a necklace of ball bearings. The design was modelled on the bamboo and wicker loungers that Le Corbusier saw in Swiss tuberculosis sanitoria.

In 1923, Le Corbusier put his ideas into print in a little book, *Vers Une Achitecture* (mistranslated into English as *Towards a New Architecture)* **bottom right**. It contained several images of cars and planes that influenced his ideas about efficiency and compactness which he applied to the home.

He was photographed sketching by René Burri in 1959 **opposite**. 'The smallest pencil stroke had to have a point,' Perriand said of her time with Le Corbusier.

SPACE AND LIGHT AND ORDER. THOSE ARE THE THINGS THAT MEN NEED JUST AS MUCH AS THEY NEED BREAD OR A PLACE TO SLEEP. – LE CORBUSIER

Sainte Marie de La Tourette is a Dominican Order priory in a valley near Lyon, France, designed by Le Corbusier in 1953 and built between 1956 and 1960. La Tourette is considered one of the more important buildings of the late modernist style. 'Create a silent dwelling for one hundred bodies and one hundred hearts,' he was instructed by the Dominican Reverend Father, Marie-Alain Couturier.

The building consists of 100 sleeping rooms for teachers and students, study halls, a recreation room, a library, a refectory and, of course, a church.

In 1998 the English designer Jasper Morrison was asked to design a chair for the refectory at La Tourette. The European oak chair he created **left** was inspired by one of the benches in the monastery's chapel, and just 100 (of course) were made. Morrison spent a night in one of the cells, 'a perfect room, where in about 10 square metres you have an apartment: when you enter the door on your right you have the bathroom and a cabinet which divides the bathroom from the bed, in which you can put from one side your clothes and from the other your book or whatever; after the bed you have a table and a chair and then in line with the door to the room there is the door to the terrace and the terrace is no more than one metre deep, but it's enough. So I had this very nice night, in a room with a lot of spirit, a lot of character, where I felt completely comfortable ... This experience made me think about the amazing power of architecture, a power that allows you to transform concrete walls, which can look like a prison if left empty, thanks to good planning, into a room which is 100 per cent comfortable and practical, where you really feel good.'

Le Corbusier's round, owl glasses were a such a characteristic part of his appearance that they have become almost emblematic of the modern architect, and it is a look that has been widely emulated **below**. At a recent exhibition of Le Corbusier's work at the Barbican Gallery in London, similar spectacles were on sale in the exhibition shop, as were a series of 'pop-art' illustrations of the Villa Savoye by Stefi Otz **below left**.

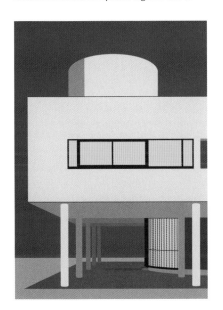

While in Britain, Breuer worked with Jack Pritchard's company Isokon creating a series of furniture pieces in bent plywood. Most memorable was his Long Chair, but the series also included tables and stacking chairs aimed at young professional couples setting up house in small spaces, who wanted to live in the modern style with as few possessions as possible. That same ideal was embraced by the architect, Wells Coates, who created the Minimum Flat, a small dwelling space kitted out with built-in furniture and a handful of simple, mass-produced furniture items. The idea of living a modern life without the burden of too many possessions appealed to many young intellectuals who sought to reject the Victorian clutter of their parents' homes.

More, more, more

Possessions, however, were not a burden in 1930s American homes, where the rational kitchen gave way to a radically different, more consumption-oriented interpretation of that domestic space. Design, seen as scientific management of domestic spaces, had focused on the organisation of the kitchen's components, with the streamlining effect of built-in furnishings; but the driving force in the design of the inter-war American kitchen was the appearance and role of the electrical goods and gadgets that were now available to help the modern housewife in the performance of her domestic tasks. No single kitchen appliance was more conspicuous at this time than the refrigerator.

Electric refrigeration was an American invention: the 'ice-box' had given way to mechanical refrigerating machines, with steam engines providing the necessary power before the advent of the electric motor. The search for a domestic mechanical refrigerator had involved a number of stages – the discovery of a suitable refrigerant, the assertion of the dominance of electricity over gas, and the means to mass produce suitable cabinets for the machine. The first models, including the first Frigidaire, like the ice-boxes on which they were modelled, were made of wood. The key developments in the evolution of the design of the modern refrigerator took place between 1923 and 1933, coinciding with the growing urbanisation and expanding consuming power of American citizens, and the mass-production potential of the large manufacturers. By the mid 1930s the electric refrigerator had become a powerful 'consumer durable', and a focus for designers who sought to create a visual identity for the different models that competed in the marketplace.

In 1926 Frigidaire, which was owned by General Motors, produced a steel refrigerator and in the following year launched its more modern-looking Monitor-Top model, so named because the compressor was positioned on the top of its metal body-shell. Through the 1930s the collaborations between Frigidaire, General Electric, Kelvinator, Westinghouse and Sears Roebuck with the new consultant industrial designers led to a number of visually impressive machines that quickly became important status symbols. The Raymond Loewy-designed Coldspot refrigerator, created for Sears Roebuck, was among the most striking of them all. Loewy used this commission to introduce the idea of annual object obsolescence into refrigerator design and new Coldspot models were launched in 1935, 1936, 1937 and 1938. Each one had more or less the same streamlined metal shell, produced by the same machines that made automobile bodies but, incrementally, new features were introduced, from a flush door handle with a recessed hole beneath it, inspired by the automobile, to a light that went on when the door was opened.

The bulbous curves and dramatic lines of the sleek-looking modern Coldspot made it a highly conspicuous and prized product and it dominated numerous stylish kitchens in the 1930s. By the 1950s kitchen appliance manufacturers had added to the visual excitement of their products by adding colours – Sherwood Green and Stratford Yellow among them – thereby enabling refrigerators to continue to behave like fashion items and to dominate the large, open-plan kitchens of the immediate post-war years.

Design in the 1930s American home increasingly focused on appliances, whose development received the same sort of treatment at the hands of the American product designers as fridges had done. Numerous gadgets rolled off production lines into the homes of housewives keen to benefit from what were promoted as their labour-saving properties. The food-mixer, the electric carving knife, the electric coffee-maker and a host of other small electrical appliances filled the American kitchen and home, which had to expand to accommodate them. Dramatic, streamlined bodies were created in objects such as Henry Dreyfuss's voluptuous Model 150 vacuum cleaner for Hoover, and W. D. Teague's 1939 vacuum cleaner for Montgomery Ward. In England Christian Barman created a striking controlled heat iron for HMV in 1936 that featured an elegant, yellow, enamelled body.

The dream home

By the post-war years many homes had become repositories for modern designed objects, from the conspicuous streamlined goods in their kitchens to the 'contemporary' furniture in their open-plan living/dining rooms. Housewives were transformed from overall-clad scientists relegated to the kitchen at the back of the house

to glamorous hostesses pushing trolleys and serving food through hatches that linked their kitchens to their dining rooms. This was the era of the modern 'dream home', an ideal that was developed first in the US but which rapidly migrated to Europe.

In the years after 1945, the design of the home became more humanised – a reaction against the austerity of the home seen merely as a machine for living in – and embraced organically and geometrically inspired shapes and abstract patterns.

By the 1950s the small, all-white laboratory kitchen had been replaced by a much more open space into which colour had made an appearance and in which the housewife performed a more visible role as a hostess rather than, as hitherto, as an efficient worker. New materials, such as the plastic laminate, Formica, brought pattern and texture into these new spaces which were advertised as being as much about family life and entertaining as they were about work.

HENRY DREYFUSS

Henry Dreyfuss (1904–1977, photographed in the 1930s, **above**) was one of the USA's leading industrial consultant designers. Like Norman Bel Geddes before him, Dreyfuss came from a background in stage design and he applied his skills of dramatisation to many products of modern life, from irons, telephones and alarm clocks to tractors and trains. By applying the aerodynamic, streamlined forms of transport to rather slower-moving – indeed, frequently static – domestic machines of the modern age Dreyfuss transformed the appearance of the home. Fridges, toasters and vacuum cleaners, among many other objects, all succumbed to the pull of the 'aesthetics of speed'.

The little iron **right** was designed by Dreyfuss for General Electric in 1948, a miniature relative – with its bulbous head and tapered rear – of his magnficent Hudson locomotive (1938) **opposite**, even though the only movement it made was up and down an ironing board. The Hudson, by contrast, was designed by Dreyfuss for the New Yok Central railroad to pull the 20th Century Limited, an express passenger train that operated between Grand Central Station in New York and LaSalle Street Station in Chicago. Twenty years later, the New York Times called it, 'the world's greatest train.'

Ten years after the steam locomotive, Dreyfuss designed the interior of the the new Pullman-Standard Dining Car **above right**, which went into service on 17 September 1948 and was the epitome of elegance, restraint and comfort.

WELL-DESIGNED, MASS-PRODUCED GOODS CONSTITUTE A NEW AMERICAN ARTFORM AND ARE RESPONSIBLE FOR THE CREATION OF A NEW AMERICAN CULTURE. THESE PRODUCTS OF THE APPLIED ARTS ARE A PART OF EVERYDAY AMERICAN LIVING AND WORKING, NOT MERELY MUSEUM PIECES TO BE SEEN ON A SUNDAY AFTERNOON. – HENRY DREYFUSS

One of Henry Dreyfuss's lasting legacies to twentieth-century design was his commitment to 'human factors' or 'anthropometrics'. Later in his career he wrote two important books on the subject, *Designing for People* (1955) and *The Measure of Man* (1960). More recently his approach has been labelled 'human-centred' design. It can be seen in the range of Oxo's Good Grips kitchen tools **above**. With the general ageing of the population much more thought is being given to the needs of users with arthritic hands who find it hard to peel potatoes or use a pair of scissors.

Dreyfuss's legacy can also be seen in the streamlined body of Christopher C. Deam's Airstream Bambi trailer **right**.

This new stylistic direction was spearheaded by numerous progressive architects and designers who looked less at the hard lines of the machine and more at the forms of the natural world. In Britain, for instance, the furniture designer Robin Day and his wife, the textile designer, Lucienne, designed hugely influential furniture pieces that used new materials such as laminated plywood and steel rod, as well as household textiles covered with abstract forms derived from nature. This retreat from the house as a machine was shared by many Scandinavian designers, who increasingly used light, indigenous woods and abstract patterns on their decorative art objects, as well as by American designers of the post-war era who used the forms of nature as a starting point for the development of a 'contemporary' visual language of the home.

The impact of the mass media in these years also ensured that the dream home quickly became a popular ideal. The concept of the 'designed' home also became fashionable and a handful of designers – from Raymond Loewy to Charles and Ray Eames – became household names. (Loewy's face featured on the cover of *Time* magazine in the US in October 1949). More and more people devoured the numerous lifestyle/decoration magazines that emerged and, as a result, the home became an ever stronger marker of upward social mobility, and its contents major status symbols. In the American suburbs this led to a huge increase in the consumption of household goods, from bulbous refrigerators, to sofas and coffee-tables inspired by the soft, abstract forms of the natural world.

The prime movers in the renewed design of the American post-war modern home included Charles Eames, Eero Saarinen, and George Nelson. They initiated a wholesale rejection of the still-popular traditional style of decoration and architecture and the widespread obsession with antiques (for which the female interior decorators were blamed). In his 1945 book, co-written with Henry Wright, *Tomorrow's House,* George Nelson described how the American public was rejecting its traditions – the 'Colonial Dream House' among them – and embracing the modern home, although he knew full well that historical styles were as popular as ever in some quarters. 'A new fashion will be created,' he wrote, 'and the public will follow.' He listed Le Corbusier and Frank Lloyd Wright as key influences, and advocated a new domestic architecture that favoured open-plan designs, open hearths, modern furniture, and lots of light, space and glass. One chapter of the book, devoted to 'organised storage', indicated that Christine Frederick's advice had not been forgotten, either. Above all, although they still incorporated an idealistic vision of the future, his designs offered a softer, more humanised vision of the modern home than had been proposed by the inter-war modernists.

Never had it so good

The later post-war years saw the emergence of many influential new retail outlets that offered increasing numbers of people the chance to bring modern design into their home by buying contemporary furniture. In Britain Terence Conran's Habitat, which quickly expanded from its first location to a number of other urban centres, opened on London's Fulham Road in 1964, offering British consumers a range of modern items sourced in France, Italy and Sweden, among other places. A couple of decades later Ingvar Kamprad's Swedish IKEA opened stores in the US, Italy, France and the UK. By the following decade its inexpensive designs had

Julius Shulman's dramatic photo shows architect Pierre Koenig's Case Study House #22 from 1960 **right**, perilously cantilevered out over the city of Los Angeles and with the life of the inhabitants exposed for all to see through the large plate glass windows. It displays both a real home in a real building, but also an ideal. This house – with its large potted plants, open space and comfortable seating – evokes the dream lifestyle that modern architects envisaged in the years after the Second World War and which consumers, at least those rich enough to afford it, willingly embraced.

brought the possibility of living with modern style within the reach of vast numbers of home-makers across the globe. Indeed, as we shall see in more detail in Chapter Five, the 1980s and 1990s saw the home resurface as *the* designed environment in which people's hopes and dreams were reflected. Increasingly the media leapt upon home design as a symbol of people's ideas about themselves, their fantasies and their aspirations. From the 1970s onwards a new emphasis upon the home as a reminder of the past joined its more progressive face. By then Laura Ashley was selling the British public domestic fabrics printed with Victorian floral patterns, whilst Martha Stewart was offering a correlative pastiche to Americans. Festoon curtains joined Venetian blinds, and architectural salvage companies sprang up everywhere to provide customers with the pine doors and Victorian mantelpieces that had been savagely ripped out of the same houses only a few years earlier, most enthusiastically in Britain but, to some extent at least, in the US and Europe as well.

Anything goes

Drawing from a variety of styles and ideas, commercial postmodernism became the design movement that dominated the 1970s and 1980s. In essence, postmodernism sought to reject the universal, highly politicised, unrelentingly forward-looking approaches of architectural and design modernism and to replace them with a more playful, even ironic and less dogmatic approach, bringing with it a new stylistic freedom and diversity. Nowhere was this more in evidence than in the design of the home. By the 1990s the new Georgian or Victorian house (lovingly restored or faithfully reproduced) sat alongside stark minimal interiors with concrete floors and granite kitchen surfaces. Magazines and television programmes presented rooms – and even houses

– as stage sets upon which designers waved their magic wands to transform rooms into a myriad of styles, none of which were judged 'better' or more appropriate than the others, although in general they were thought to be successful if they expressed the identities of the people living in them. This represented a significant break with the beliefs of the modernists who had set out to ensure that function and materials alone determined the nature and appearance of home, and that simply designed interiors could, with the help of mass production, be made available to everyone. The bourgeois individualism that they had hoped to overturn had clearly survived and the idea that people would learn to live efficient lives with as few possessions as possible was never realised. The post-modern age resisted all attempts at social engineering. There were no longer any rights or wrongs, no good or bad taste, not good or bad design, only appropriate expression.

Even the modernist minimal interior was transformed into just another stylistic option in the marketplace, and Elsie de Wolfe's idea that homes are places in which people express themselves won out in the end. By the end of

In the years following the Second World War kitchen gadgets became more and more popular and possessing them was considered to mark their owners out as chic and modern. This was particularly true for women, at whom these products were aimed. In the early 1960s Moulinex **above** promised that its kitchen and other domestic appliances would 'liberate woman'.

By the early twenty-first century the appeal of 'home-making', and its relationship with people's (especially women's) identities and everyday lives may have reached a peak in teenage girls' obsession with the interactive computer game, the Sims **opposite**, which permits them to create a whole family, its lifestyle scenarios and the domestic environment in which those scenarios are played out. Replacing the traditional dolls' house, which left more to the imagination, the Sims is all-encompassing, permitting its players to choose everything from clothes to bed linen.

IT IS NO LONGER POSSIBLE, EVEN TO PEOPLE OF ONLY FAINTLY AESTHETIC TASTES, TO BUY CHAIRS MERELY TO SIT UPON OR A CLOCK MERELY THAT IT SHOULD TELL THE TIME. HOME-MAKERS ARE DETERMINED TO HAVE THEIR HOUSES, OUTSIDE AND IN, CORRECT ACCORDING TO THE BEST STANDARDS.
– ELSIE DE WOLFE

the twentieth century consumption had defeated production as the driving force of design. In the early twenty-first century the design of the home continues to contain and express the same meanings it did in the middle of the nineteenth century, although now for many more people. The home continues to be the destiny for most designed consumer goods, from sofas to electrical appliances to computers. Once in the home, however, consumers have the freedom to arrange them as they wish. Only in the private space of the home can people still create their own personal aesthetic, functional and psychological spaces. In a world in which the design of goods is largely pre-determined it is a freedom that is highly valued and widely exercised. If the continuing growth of the media's involvement with the design of domestic spaces is anything to go by – from make-over shows and voyeuristic visits to the homes of the rich and famous, to how-to-do-it in your own homes and the expansion of popular home magazines of all sorts and sizes, it is a freedom that we are going to continue to exploit for some years to come.

THE CHAIR: TUBULAR STEEL

Tubular steel is lightweight, strong and can be bent into a number of forms. Its use was fundamental to the design of one of the great modernist innovations – the cantilever chair, which has no back legs.

Marcel Breuer **above** was inspired by the comfort of armchairs in men's clubs and by the strength and lightness of the bent tubular steel of his bicycle handlebars when he created what came to be called his Wassily armchair in 1925, named after his Bauhaus colleague, Wassily Kandinsky. The chair can be seen – alongside Breuer's Laccio side table – at the Bauhaus in Dessau **opposite**.

The first bent tubular steel cantilevered chair was designed by the Dutch architect, urban planner and designer Mart Stam in 1926 **top right** using lengths of gas-pipe fittings. Both Marcel Breuer and Mies van der Rohe emulated his success with their own versions of this chair type: Breuer created his B32 cantilevered bent tubular steel Cesca chair (available with or without arms) **bottom right** when he was at the Bauhaus in 1928. He added strong wooden-framed cane panels for the back and the seat, thereby eliminating the need for any additional structural elements.

The British designer Ross Lovegrove created his Magic chair **middle right** in 1997. It is a startlingly innovative design and a feat of engineering as groundbreaking as the cantilever chair was in its day. The seat appears to hover in space with no support to keep it from tipping over as it is only fastened to the tubular steel legs at a fixing point midway up the chair back.

ELECTRIC SERVANTS

The advent of electricity into the home was transforming. The incandescent light bulb of Thomas Edison **above** illuminated domestic interiors (and revealed much more dirt than gas lighting). Advances were especially strong in the US where housework was more likely to be done by the woman of the house rather than by servants. Some labour-saving devices simply replaced manual labour, but others rethought the whole process involved, such as vacuum cleaners that sucked in dirt where brooms had swept it away By the 1950s **left** the kitchen was transformed from laboratory to the 'heart of the home', a place where the hostess could entertain her guests surrounded by the latest built-in electrical appliances.

The KitchenAid mixer **top right** is emblematic of domestic homemaking, its unchanged retro styling redolent of a mythic past in which cakes were freshly baked and bread brought warm to the table, no doubt to be toasted in the equally retro Dualit **middle left**. The German white goods manufacturer, Miele **top left**, has positioned itself as a byword for state-of-the-art efficiency, with a price tag to match, while a Maytag refrigerator **middle right** – though relatively common in the US – is a status symbol in European kitchens, where space is often at a premium.

What was once cutting edge can date, however: the British designer, James Dyson, has seen his bagless vacuum cleaner copied by other manufacturers, but the DC25 Dyson Ball **bottom left** puts a spin – almost literally – on conventional design by doing away with fixed wheels. Michael Graves's electric kettle for Alessi **bottom right** – more commonly seen as a hob-top version – is no longer the *dernier cri* of postmodern kitchens that it once was.

ARTICULATED LAMPS

Before electricity, light cast its light according to the brightness of a flame. The idea that lighting could be controlled was largely unthought of, and early electric lighting remained relatively static. The family-owned Terry Spring Company has continually produced Anglepoise lamps since George Carwardine invented them in 1932. The classic, aluminium 1227 **right** directs light much as a human arm would position the source of light to illuminate its purpose, and is found in homes and offices all over the world. Like many long-lasting design icons it could be said to have been 'engineered' as Cawardine was a car designer whose expertise lay in vehicle suspension systems. He set out to design a task light that could be positioned flexibly and would remain in the positions in which it was put. To that end he developed a system of jointed metal rods and springs attached at one end to a heavy base and at the other a shaded light bulb. Its first use was in working environments, such as workshops, offices and doctors' surgeries but it gradually found itself in the home as well. Its workmanlike, functional appearance endeared it to modernist designers and archiects who embraced the maxim of 'form follows function'.

Part of the charm of the Anglepoise is its anthropomorphic design, most famously celebrated in Pixar Animation's charming ident. Not everyone has viewed the design so benignly: in 1949, the BBC's Michael Standing

issued an edict banning its use in the belief that a man working with light from only an Anglepoise would harbour illicit thoughts and consequently produce degenerate material.

Since then, work lighting has evolved with developments in engineering and production techniques. Richard Sapper's elegant Tizio task light **left** became, in the 1970s and 1980s, as ubiquitous as the Anglepoise before it. Its deceptively simple mechanism and balancing system enabled it to be extremely flexible and it added a modern design feature to countless offices. Michele de Lucchi and Giancarlo

Fassina's Tolomeo light for Artemide **top left**, produced from 1987, has become a 'new classic'. Its brushed aluminium shade and structure and self-effacing form is both non-obtrusive and functional .

Herman Miller's highly sculptural, LED Leaf lamp (2006) **opposite** takes task light into new territory. Designed by Yves Behar of fuseproject it was the first to offer both mood lighting for intimate, non-work situations and a cooler light for working environments, controlled by a sliding wheel control on the base, similar to that of an Apple iPod.

LET SLIP THE
DOGS OF WAR

DESIGN IN WARTIME

Shiny new gadgets like Raymond Loewy's swollen Coldspot refrigerator took pride of place in the kitchens of the newly rich inhabitants of America's 1930s suburbs. However, when the Second World War began at the end of that decade, design's preoccupation with the creation of status symbols for aspiring consumers was suddenly irrelevant. Instead, designers had to turn their attentions to basic human needs and their nation's survival. It was their skills in communication and product innovation that were in demand, while their talents for creating exotic fashionable styles were left, temporarily, on the back burner.

Design, in countries that are at war, finds a completely different role. War highlights the importance of life and death, and the struggle simply to survive. In this situation the luxury of self-expression and the fulfilment of desire become secondary considerations. More prosaically, war also diminishes the market-led purpose of design. In their new role, designers made a number of important contributions during the years of the Second World War and immediately after it. The skills of graphic designers were needed to get important messages across to populations at large; product designers were called upon to design the few consumer goods that were still needed, although with the state controlling their manufacture; in their capacity as inventor-engineers designers created the machines and paraphernalia of war itself; and they were indispensable in the process of turning war-time developments into peace-time goods and environments.

Design changed its focus dramatically in the interlude between the tantalizing promises of a utopian future offered at the 1939–40 New York World's Fair and the renewed optimism of the 1951 Festival of Britain. Designers responded strongly to the call to work for the war effort, from creating propaganda campaigns, working in camouflage and on the Utility furniture and clothing project in Britain, to designing machines and objects for war itself – from tanks to aircraft to bombs. Designers also played an important role in making the transition from war to peace, whether by re-using materials – metals, plastics and moulded plywood – in a new context, or by taking war-time technologies and products into a new era. Hitler's support for the Volkswagen car (later the VW Beetle), for example, led to a post-war automotive success story, while the Jeep and the Land Rover found significant civilian markets in the years after 1945. The story of the computer also has a war-to-peace component to it, while new developments in housing and mass-produced furniture answered the demands of post-war populations in a number of countries.

The boundaries, in war-time, between engineering, invention and design were very fine ones as individuals, working within the tight utilitarian and performance constraints of war, often crossed from one activity to another, seeing them as part of the same continuum. They used their creative powers to push technology and invention to their limits and, as a result, sometimes by chance, they frequently succeeded in developing what have since come to be classic, iconic designs.

The British artist, Peter Kennard, made a lot of work for the Campaign for Nuclear Disarmament in the late 1970s and early '80s, including the Hay-wain with Cruise Missile photomontage (1981) **previous pages**, which disrupts Constables's bucolic idyll with nuclear missiles and a soldier throwing a hand-grenade. 'The point of my work,' he explained, 'is to use easily recognisable iconic images, but to render them unacceptable.'

As advertisers know only too well, posters can be an incredibly effective means to propagating a message, the simpler the better **opposite**. A 1937 poster designed by Hans Breidenstein with photography by Dr Paul Wolff **top left** promotes the Aryan idyll of Nordensee, a resort of the North Sea I Prussia, complete with fluttering swastikas, whereas workers from Vichy France are assured that, 'While working in Germany you will be the ambassador of French quality,' **top right** in a poster from 1943 attributed to Raoul Eric Castel. A similar appeal to national pride is made by Howard Lieberman's United We Win poster **below left** from the US in 1942, whereas the one from the USSR in 1943, designed by N. Shukhov and Victor Semenovich Klimashin **below right**, exhorts the populace to, 'Beat the German Beasts! The destruction of Hitler's army is possible and necessary.'

Building the world of tomorrow

The US entered the Second World War in 1941, following the Japanese attack on Pearl Harbor. Only two years earlier it had been celebrating its achievements in technology and design, and looking forward to an optimistic future in which those two forces would take America to a new level of material affluence. 'Building the World of Tomorrow' was the main theme of the 1939–40 New York World's Fair. The industrial designer, rather than the architect, was the hero here, who envisaged where the products and processes of modern civilisation were leading America. As Walter Dorwin Teague explained, 'Because the industrial designers ... understand public taste and [are] able to speak in a popular tongue as a profession they are bound to ... think in terms of today and tomorrow, it was natural that the Board of Design should turn to them for the planning of the major exhibits.' Teague himself designed the Ford, US Steel, Eastman Kodak and National Cash Register pavilions at the Fair.

Product streamlining influenced the style of the temporary pavilions, and smooth, rounded surfaces were widely employed. The 700-foot Trylon and the 200-foot Perisphere dominated the event. Vivid colour was used in the avenues that radiated out from the white centre, each one taking on a darker hue as it moved towards the periphery. Henry Dreyfuss designed the Perisphere's interior exhibit, The City of the Future. Transport featured strongly at the Fair with an emphasis on the future role of the new road and rail systems. Raymond Loewy's Transport of Tomorrow exhibit featured a streamlined taxi, a liner, cars and trucks, as well as a rocket-ship that was predicted to travel between New York and London in 1960. Norman Bel Geddes showed the results of his transportation experiments in the General Motors Building. Highways and Horizons, his exhibit, envisaged a network of motorways covering the US. Together the industrial designers created a popular, futuristic fantasy, projected forward from the technological and design advances already achieved, and it captured the public's imagination in an unprecedented way. Little did they know that, before that dream could be realised, the world was to experience a hiatus during which all progress would be re-focused into a new direction, namely victory in war.

The New York World's Fair took place between April and October in 1939 and between the same months again in 1940. It covered a vast 492 hectares/1,216 acres in Flushing Meadows in Queens, and was a hugely ambitious and forward-looking event aimed at bringing a burst of optimism into the Depression years. Its opening slogan was, 'Dawn of a New Day', and the Fair focused on the future-gazing work of the emergent consultant designers who envisaged new objects of transport and other tools for modern living aimed at the American public. This poster **above left** shows the symbolic Trylon that stood 210 metres/700 feet high and the spherical Perisphere, 60 metres/200 feet in diameter, which housed an exhibit called The World of Tomorrow. Both were covered with white gypsum and formed part of the Theme Center, designed by Wallace Anderson and J. Andre Fouilhoux, with interior exhibits designed by Henry Dreyfuss. The Road of Tomorrow **right** was part of the Ford Pavilion in the Transportation Zone and was designed by Walter Dorwin Teague, known as the Dean of industrial design at the time. In spite of its futuristic optimism, by the time the Fair reopened in 1940 its theme was changed to 'For Peace and Freedom' to reflect the escalation of war in Europe.

ABRAM GAMES

Abram Games (1914–1996) was a member of the group of graphic designers who made an enormous impact on the British public during the war years with their striking and highly innovative posters. Linked to the war effort in a variety of ways, Games succeeded in developing a poster style that combined the shock tactics of the Surrealist artists with an original and immediate visual language that depicted the imperatives of war for the population at large.

The son of immigrants, the largely self-taught Games became the official poster artist to the British War Office during the Second World War. His best known work was a recruitment poster for the ATS (known as the 'Blonde Bombshell') just one of many popular posters – although the Army banned it, replacing his lipstick- wearing 'bombshell' with a more wholesome country girl.

This Child Found a Blind (1943) **left** directly links the danger of leaving unexploded ammunition on practice sites to their shocking consequences. A child's coffin gradually transforms into an arrow that points to a grenade, the cause of her death. Seen from a distance, the black grenade becomes an exclamation mark: 'If ideas do not work when they are an inch high, they are never going to work,' Games said.

Your Britain, Fight for it Now (1942) **below** was commissioned by the Army Bureau of Current Affairs to be issued to the forces as a focus for the 'just cause' of war. It juxtaposes the miserable reality of wartorn Britain with a post-war vision of modern schools (and, in other posters in the same series, of social housing and public health centres). Its overt left-wing sympathies incurred the wrath of members of the British War Cabinet.

Our Jungle Fighters Want Socks, Please Knit Now **right** is a witty and cleverly constructed poster that encouraged civilians to get knitting and provided them with information about where they could acquire patterns and wool. The green haze and tangle of wool effectively represent the conditions in the jungles of Asia, whilst the two knitting needles are a graphic representation of a soldier marching, his feet protected by newly knitted socks.

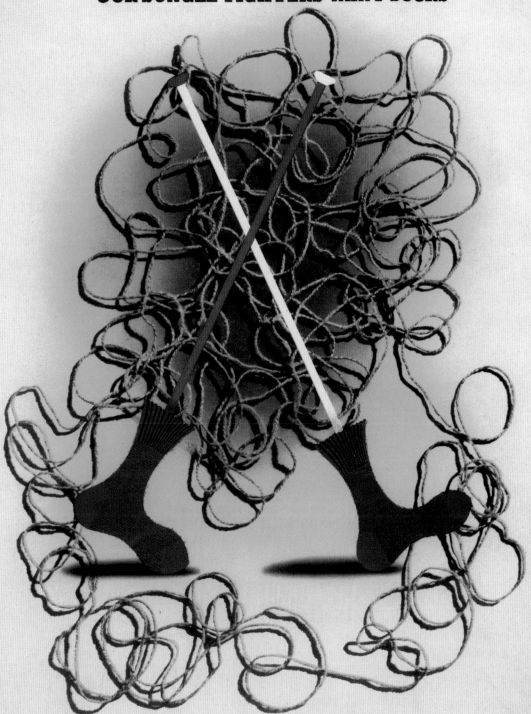

FUCK
THE DRAFT

I WIND THE SPRING AND THE PUBLIC, IN LOOKING AT THE POSTER, WILL HAVE THAT SPRING RELEASED. – ABRAM GAMES

The graphic language and immediacy of propaganda posters make a direct appeal for an emotional rather than an intellectual response. In the post-war years, these posters have become an effective tool for 'counter-cultural' organisations, from the peace movement to anti-vivisectionists.

Fuck the Draft (1969) **opposite** is explicit in word and picture. The work of an anonymous designer in the US, it shows a young man burning his draft papers in protest at the war in Vietnam, and bears witness to the continued potency of posters – now using photography – to communicate simple messages very powerfully.

In 2004, a series of political posters based on Apple's iPod campaign began appearing first in New York and soon after in Los Angeles. The most iconic uses the silhouette of an Iraqi prisoner held and tortured in Abu Ghraib **left**. The posters are the work of two design collectives, Copper Green in New York and Forkscrew Graphics in LA and they appeared on a website that asked people to download them as a means of disseminating a message to as large an audience as possible. Its reference to the iPod campaign demonstrates the close links that exist with commercial advertising. Whether consciously or not, Forkscrew echo the sentiments of the Vietnam poster when, on their website, they instruct, 'It's about two feet by three feet of freedom. Download it. Propagate it. Get involved. And then do something else all your own. We don't give a fuck.'

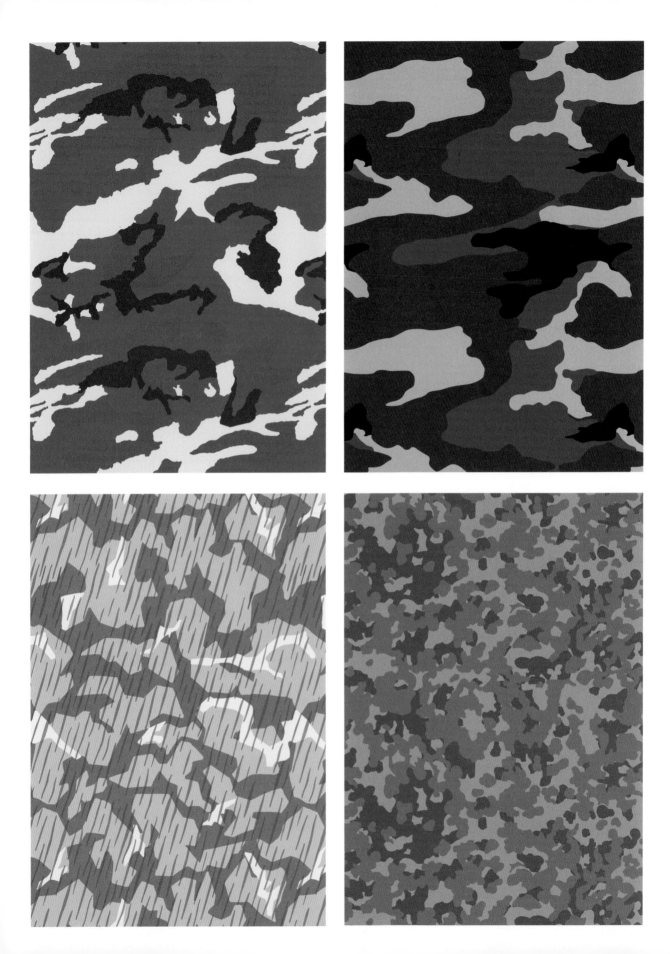

Getting the message across

The beginning of the war, in September 1939, initiated a period of six years during which the world was to change beyond all recognition. Design inevitably changed as well, transferring its focus from the commercial marketplace to the national war effort. In a number of countries the skills of graphic designers were, as they had been in the First World War, applied to the powerful and evocative tools of propaganda – posters, leaflets and so on – to communicate government information directly and memorably.

In Germany, designers often used modernist images. A striking poster from 1940, for example, featuring heavily stylised tanks, air-borne fighter planes and the profiled head of a helmeted soldier accompanied by text in a sans-serif typeface which aimed to recruit Dutchmen to the Waffen-SS following the occupation of the Netherlands, while another, from 1944, was used to try to recruit British prisoners of war into the German army. A similar phenomenon occurred in other countries including the US and Canada. The Canadian government undertook an extensive propaganda campaign which included over seven hundred posters. Photographs were widely used, especially those of glamorous, Hollywood-style housewives being exhorted to support the war effort, and of square-jawed, thin-lipped helmetted soldiers in action.

Many British designers, especially graphic and advertising artists, offered their talents to the Ministry of Information (MoI). Several established their reputations during the war and went on to be key establishment designers in the post-war era owing to the highly innovative uses of imagery and techniques that they developed in their propaganda work. They included Tom Eckersley, who created posters for the MoI while he was a cartographer for the Royal Air Force from 1940 to 1945, and Abram Games who joined the infantry in 1940, but was called to the War Office the following year to create a recruiting poster for the Royal Armoured Corps. He went on to design some of the Second World War's most memorable images. In 1942 he was appointed Official War Office Poster Designer. (He went on to design the logo for the 1951 Festival of Britain, held on London's South Bank.) Milner Gray was the MoI's head of exhibitions from 1940 to 1941, and he subsequently became a founding member of the Design Research Unit, Britain's first, US-style, design consultancy. These men all played hugely important roles in the British war effort, acting as powerful communicators at a time when it was vital that the right messages were sent in the right way to the right people at the right time.

Advertising in reverse

The skills of artists and designers were called on to create camouflage in its various forms. The development of aerial surveillance in the First World War had meant that guns, equipment and buildings had had to be hidden from view. Dazzle ships, for example, developed by the English painter, Norman Wilkinson, were developed to confuse German U-boats, and papier mâché heads had been strategically positioned in trenches. The French military had taken the lead in the field, using the skills of the Cubist painters, while the Germans had also contributed, notably through their application of pattern to the surfaces of their famous 'coal-skuttle' metal helmets. By the Second World War camouflage techniques had become much more sophisticated. Dummy tanks, made of wood and cardboard, and fake landing craft were constructed to deceive the enemy, along with other decoys. Designers developed patterns, often with origins in the natural and animal worlds, for military uniforms to help

Camouflage has long been a powerful weapon – or defence – in nature, but it was only in the twentieth century that military camouflage became widely used **opposite**. Before that, armies used bright colours and bold armour, which were intended to identify their own troops and intimidate the enemy. Different patterns and colours opposite are used according to the battle environment, from jungle to desert to sea.

It is not only people, planes, tanks and ships that camouflage is used to conceal from the enemy: a member of the 137th Armoured Division of the US Army displays his camouflaged Bible **left** following a Christian church service in Baghdad in 2003.

troops, whether in deserts or swamps or in the snow, to move with minimum visibility.

Several leading British architects and designers were asked to use their skills in the creation of camouflage during the Second World War. Among them were the architects Basil Spence and Hugh Casson, the theatre designer Oliver Messel, and the future Rector of the Royal College of Art, Richard Guyatt. Christopher Frayling has written of Guyatt that, 'During the Second World War, he was recruited by the camouflage directorate to help hide Scotland's factories from the Luftwaffe, a sort of advertising in reverse. Much of his time was spent in aerial reconnaissance, crouched in the hull of a Sunderland flying boat, sketching possible targets in pastel with a view to blending them into their surrounding landscapes.'

Resourceful design
Resources became scarce during wartime in many countries (and continued to be so after the war ended) and design played a major part in dealing

During the Second World War most factories ceased producing goods for civilians and went over to manufacturing for war. One British exception was the Utility scheme that provided newly weds and people with bombed-out homes with the furniture and other goods they needed. Everything was available, from chairs and tables to items of kitchen equipment. At the opening of a Utility furniture exhibition **above** Government minister Arthur Greenwood is shown a Utility mixing bowl. The chairs, just visible, show how the Utility scheme drew on traditional Windsor chair designs and reflected a workmanlike, vernacular approach to design and manufacture.

The idea of simple, easily constructed objects has remained in place ever since and is reflected in these Screw side tables **right**, designed by Tom Dixon in 2009 as part of his new Utility range. The table is made from a bombproof, cast-iron tripod with a marble top, whilst the industrial-strength aluminium screw allows for multiple heights by simply spinning the top. The strong industrial look openly celebrates both the means of manufacture and the functionality.

with these problems. In many countries, such as the US, war caused various industries to work in new areas. Among other initiatives the War Wood Industries was formed to oversee the production of wood manufacturing for government contracts. In 1943, for example, the Chicago-based Butler Specialty Company produced twelve thousand beds while S. Karpe and Co. made plywood chests, and the Tonk Manufacturing Company made wooden casings for lead-lined ammunition storage boxes. The shift of manufacturing from domestic goods to war production posed a problem for people in real need of items for their homes.

In Britain, the problem had an inventive solution. The 'Utility' scheme brought a limited range of consumer items – furniture, household goods and clothing – to the people who most needed them, primarily young married couples, the owners of bombed out houses and people in the services. Driven by need, not consumer desire, Utility products were designed to be independent of notions of fashion. As the name of the scheme suggested, they were meant to be useful first and foremost. Utility furniture was linked to the shortage of timber and the need to regulate production and consumption.

The idea was first mooted by Hugh Dalton, the president of the Board of Trade, who brought in the furniture designer Gordon Russell to help develop it. The aim was to produce a limited set of simple, standardised items at a controlled price. Britain's predicament and the government's commitment to fair distribution – what has been called 'war socialism' – meant that there was an opportunity to put William Morris's ideals into action. Russell was linked to the Arts & Crafts Movement and he saw, in the Utility project, a chance to realise some of its principles – a design project which had real needs and social idealism, rather than market-led values, at its heart.

Back in 1937 the British Council for Art and Industry had already discussed the possibility of making 'good design' available to everyone. Now in 1942 the Utility Furniture Committee was set up, on which Russell served, and it asked a group of designers to make proposals for a range of furniture which would fulfil Dalton's ambition to 'secure the production of furniture of good, sound construction in simple but agreeable designs and at reasonable prices.' The designs of Edwin L. Clinch and H.T. Cutler, who were linked to the traditional High Wycombe furniture industry, were finally selected. In October that year an exhibition of Utility furniture in a number of room settings was opened to the public and, in 1943, a Utility furniture catalogue was published.

The Utility furniture items were simple wooden pieces that recalled traditional, vernacular designs, albeit with a modern twist. Ladder-backed dining chairs were combined with new versions of Windsor chairs, for example. The cabinets – a sideboard and a chest of drawers among them – were basic, solid items with no frills. The Arts & Crafts influence was clear, especially in the names of some of the later pieces – a 1946 mahogany occasional table was called 'Cotswold', for example, while a dining table of the same year was dubbed 'Chiltern'. Russell was very clear that he was using the Utility project to realise Morris's ideals. 'I felt', he wrote 'that to raise the whole standard of furniture for the mass of the people was not a bad job. And it has always seemed to me that, when in doubt as to people's requirements, to aim at giving them something better than they might be expected to demand … surely it might be possible to use the Utility specification as the basis of a quality mark.' Russell's idealism underpinned the whole project, ensuring that a standard was set and maintained. This was state-controlled design at its most influential and effective.

After the hostilities, however, such was human nature that people inevitably became bored with the functional simplicity of the Utility ranges – which were, it must be said, often a little bland and anonymous. By the 1950s the fashionable 'Contemporary' style, with its bright colours and patterned textiles and wallpapers, had emerged to satisfy the need for something new. Indeed the consumer response to Utility furniture, illustrates an important lesson: using design as a tool for social control can produce designs that fail to offer the variety and the capacity for individual expression that is often supplied by designers fulfilling the demands of the marketplace.

The furniture scheme was not Utility's only achievement, however; it also ventured into clothing, textiles and household goods. The textile designer Enid Marx took over responsibility for furnishing fabrics. The constraints on design were severe – for example the repeats had to be small and only a limited number of yarns could be used – but Marx was able to create a number of striking patterns, including 'Spot and Stripe' and 'Chevron'. The clothing, again constrained by a restricted amount of material, was designed by members of the Incorporated Society of London Fashion Designers, which included Hardy Amies and Norman Hartnell. The clothes looked highly utilitarian – jackets could only have three buttons and there could be no additional trimming – but they also betrayed some signs of being inspired by contemporary fashion, especially in their pinched waists and large reveres. While they aspired to universality, in hindsight they can clearly be seen as products of their time. They also bore a strong resemblance to women's military uniform, especially that of the ATS. Both featured reveres, front buttoning, belted waists, and skirts reaching to just below the knee. Both conveyed practicality and commonsense and

avoided any conspicuous stylishness or obvious adherence to fashion.

All over Europe and America, wartime hardships and restrictions kept clothing styles utilitarian, parsimonious with material, and often rather drab. After the war, people were hungry for glamour. When the French couturier Dior launched his elegant 'New Look' in 1947, it dramatically confirmed the need for a break from the severe designs and regulations of wartime clothing. His collection of luxurious clothes with soft shoulders, hour-glass waists and full flowing skirts promoted a new femininity in fashionable dress and a celebration of flair and romance.

The Utility scheme embraced dress as well as furniture, thereby providing ordinary people with a complete set of simple, functional lifestyle accessories that circumvented fashion for the most part. This worsted Utility suit in royal blue wool with a full skirt from 1950 **above** went some way towards meeting the fashion requirements of the post-war era when more fabric was available. The light-hearted stance of the model suggests the optimism of post-war years.

This striking Polish poster **right**, designed by Roman Cieslewicz, promotes Polish fashion from the late 1950s and could have been created by the Surrealist artists several decades earlier. It equally dispels the myth that life behind the Iron Curtain was uniformly grey. The huge rose that is displayed on a mannequin with bold features that contrast sharply with it, while the black background adds to the dramatic effect.

moda polska

ROSIE THE RIVETER

STEEL WORKER

AUGUST 9, 1943 **10** CENTS
YEARLY SUBSCRIPTION $4.50

REG. U. S. PAT. OFF.

With so many men called to war, there was a critical shortage of manpower in factories. Propaganda in print, film and radio was used to conscript women into manufacturing. Rosie the Riveter was the fictional epitome of this new breed of women in a man's world. Norman Rockwell's painting of Rosie sold at Sotheby's in 2002 for almost $5 million, but Rosie's most iconic manifestation is in J. Howard Miller's 'We Can Do It!' poster (1942) **above**. Women were encouraged to put their femininity temporarily to one side in an effort to maximise their physical strength and working skills. The cover of *Life* magazine (1943) **right** depicts a begoggled female steel worker welding a piece of metal in the Gary Armor Plate Plant of the Carnegie-Illinois Steel Corporation in Indiana, which undoubtedly ended up as part of a ship or an aeroplane. Real-life women riveters **opposite** work inside an aircraft's fuselage. In all three images the women depicted have thrown off conventional ideals of the feminine for the war effort, covering their hair and wearing utilitarian work clothes to take on the heavy production work that was required of them when the men went off to war.

Rosie has since become a feminist icon, but the slogan, 'Do the job he left behind,' said a lot. She could do it as long as he did not want it or was not around to do it. As soon as soldiers began to return home, women were forced out of these jobs.

WE'D NEVER HAD ANY OPPORTUNITY TO DO THAT KIND OF WORK. DO YOU THINK THAT IF YOU DID DOMESTIC WORK ALL OF YOUR LIFE ... AND YOU FINALLY GOT A CHANCE WHERE YOU CAN GET A DIGNIFIED JOB, YOU WOULDN'T FLY THROUGH THE DOOR? – LYN CHILDS, THE LIFE AND TIMES OF ROSIE THE RIVETER (1980)

WHEN I JOINED CUSTER I DONNED THE UNIFORM OF A SOLDIER. IT WAS A BIT AWKWARD AT FIRST BUT I SOON GOT TO BE PERFECTLY AT HOME IN MEN'S CLOTHES. – CALAMITY JANE

Uniforms for women, especially in wartime or in military service, typically degender their wearer, but designers have since played with and subverted these stereotypes.

In the 1950s and '60s, airlines typically recruited young, attractive women in airline livery to market their product, including the model Felicity Downer **above** wearing the British United Airways air stewardess uniform at Gatwick Airport in the mid 1960s.

Chinese fashion designer Hoi Lam Wong won Collection Of The Year at the 2009 London College of Fashion degree show for her collection **right** that turns femininity on its head by mixing masculine tailoring and uniforms such as this jumpsuit with floral prints, sequins and work boots.

These subversions of gender, uniform and identity are played out in complex and powerful ways by the Libyan designer, Basma Ebara. His camouflage collection **opposite** worn by Libyan model Shaima in Tripoli (2007) challenges social and political norms.

Means to an end

While war-time needs gave design a role in the development of a limited number of state-regulated consumer-oriented goods, its key focus was in developing products and machines for the activity of war itself. The planes, ships, tanks, guns and bombs used in the Second World War were all designed objects with clearly defined purposes and requirements that needed high-level engineering and functional results.

Some war machines and objects stand out above others in terms of the innovative solutions provided by their design. One example is the Soviet T-34 tank, designed by Mikhail Koshkin, and produced between 1940 and 1958. The T-34 was developed both before and during the Second World War and incorporated some American and German advances, among them the suspension system of the American Christie tank. The tank had a number of defining features, including its enhanced firepower and the fact that its design focused on the ease of manufacture rather than on the comfort of its users – the crew were very cramped and it was very noisy. It was a very simple design, however, and therefore simple both to manufacture and to repair – by the end of 1945 over 57,000 had been built. Visually, it was, like Singer's first sewing machine (page 48), a fairly crude, utilitarian object whose form revealed its means of manufacture. However, in an excellent example of form following function, its appearance was highly effective: with its wide base and heavy, sloping armour, it succeeded in looking both powerful and aggressive. It apparently shocked the Germans when they first saw it in 1941. The T-34 was also very fast in action, extremely mobile in adverse conditions, such as deep mud and snow, and it could be replicated very quickly in the Kharkiv Tractor factory in the Ukraine which was located at a safe distance from German bombing. It was the most-produced tank in the Second World War and it proved itself to be a very efficient fighting machine.

To counter the unexpected success of the T-34, the German Tiger 1 tank was designed, by Henschel & Sohn, to different specifications. Equipped with the formidable 88mm gun and with armour so thick it was exceptionally difficult to attack, the Tiger was the most powerful tank in the world when it was introduced in 1942. However, the heaviness of its design sacrificed mobility, and it was much more expensive and took much longer to produce than the T-34, both crucial shortcomings in wartime.

War in the skies

Command of the air was vital in the Second World War and the British excelled at aircraft design. The Spitfire, one of the finest fighter planes of its day, was designed by Reginald Mitchell, chief designer and later technical director of Supermarine Aviation Works, who specialised in the construction of seaplanes. Between 1920 and 1936 Mitchell created over 24 different designs, among them the Southampton and Stranraer flying boats for the Royal Air Force, several of which won the Schneider Trophy, an annual air-speed competition. Because of Mitchell's success in developing high-speed aircraft, in 1930 the Air Ministry asked Supermarine to design a new fighter plane. Mitchell created first the less successful type 224 and then the type 300, the basis of his subsequent Spitfire that first took to the air in 1936; he died the following year.

The Spitfire's key characteristic was its thin, elliptically shaped wing which, along with the stressed skin construction of its curved body, gave it a distinctive silhouette. The Spitfire had a monocoque (a skin or outer shell that supports a load – as opposed to having an internal frame)

LET SLIP THE DOGS OF WAR

The Soviet T34 tank was crude but highly threatening. Designed for ease of repair rather than for the comfort of its users it was a basic killing machine whose utilitarian character made it both look and appear deadly. Its brutal, lethal efficiency ensured that the T34 tank remained a staple of the Soviet war machine in the 1950s and beyond: in 1953 it was used to quell 100,000 rioting workers in East Berlin **opposite**. Martial law was subsequently declared and T34 tanks patrolled the city, creating a menacing presence as they moved through the streets.

Germany's Tiger tank was a more advanced design than its Soviet equivalent, its engineering less crude in many ways and more comfortable for the crew and easier to operate. Its enormous gun and strong emphasis on utility gave it an aggressive character nonetheless. Although it has been described as one of the most memorable fighting machines of the mid-twentieth century, its refined engineering hindered mass production. This Tiger 1 tank **left** was used by the Italians against the landing of Allied forces in Sicily in 1943.

fuselage which allowed its interior to be unobstructed by struts or wires. While strikingly beautiful, the shape of the wings was, in fact, the result of a design solution to an engineering problem: the need to solve the conflicting requirements of being thin enough to reduce drag but having enough room, where the wings joined the fuselage, to retract the undercarriage, as well as to house the weapons and ammunition. Part of the Spitfire's design success was due to an innovative spar boom made up of five square concentric tubes that fitted into each other to make a strong but lightweight structure. The plane's fin and tailplane mirrored the shape of the wings and enhanced its aerodynamic qualities. With war looming the government paid for a new factory in Birmingham to supplement Spitfire production in Southampton. The plane played a key role in winning the Battle of Britain in 1940.

Another pioneering British designer who contributed to the progress of the war in the skies was Barnes Wallis, most famous for the bouncing bomb used in the Dambusters raid of 1943, although he also designed the huge and effective Tallboy and Grand Slam 'earthquake' bombs. But his most significant achievement was the first use of geodesic design in engineering. Wallis began his career with Vickers in airship design where he introduced what he called the geodetic construction, a curved metal lattice-framework which produced a light structure with remarkable strength. A series of bomber aircraft made by Vickers used Wallis's geodetic design, including the Wellington, whose load-bearing structure could tolerate a lot of damage. There were numerous instances – many preserved in dramatic photographs taken at the time – of Wellington bombers losing large parts of their fuselage after taking direct hits yet surviving well enough to fly home safely.

The plywood revolution

Fuselages in some other planes, such as the Loughhead S-1 and the de Havilland Mosquito, were constructed from moulded plywood, a material that came into its own in wartime owing to the search for different ways of processing timber now that it was in short supply. The pioneering American designer Charles Eames went on to use this material to produce a number of iconic designs. In 1941, with his wife and design partner Ray whom he married in that year, Eames set up a home-made moulding machine in the back room of their Los Angeles home, bringing back wood and glue from his job as a set designer for MGM to work with. In the previous year he had submitted a series of chairs – co-designed with Eero Saarinen, a colleague from the Cranbrook Academy – to a competition held by New York's Museum of Modern Art, entitled Organic Design in Home Furnishings. They were awarded first prize for their seating and for some pieces of living room furniture. The chairs featured moulded plywood shells covered with foam rubber padding and upholstery fabric. Eames had wanted to join the legs to the shell using cycle-welding, but, because the process was restricted to military applications during the war, was unable to do so. However, this work led to the Eameses being asked to contribute to the war effort. In 1942 the US Navy commissioned five thousand moulded plywood leg splints for injured airmen from them. The Eameses produced a handsome, curved lightweight splint, and later went on to make other items for the navy. Military technology, materials and cash enabled them to perfect their moulding techniques and to move to better accommodation.

In 1946 Eames and Saarinen exhibited new furniture at the Museum of Modern Art; this was produced by the Herman Miller Company.

Aircraft recognition cards were issued to civil defence officers and civilians during the Second World War to assist them in distinguishing Allied planes from enemy ones. The cards showed silhouettes of the front, carriage and side views of the aircraft, but with no identifying text. The planes could be memorised from the keys **opposite** and the cards used for guessing games and other kinds of card games such as Happy Families.

The principle was applied by the US military in 2003 to a set of playing cards depicting Iraq's Most Wanted **left** played Aces high with Sadam Hussein as the Ace of Spades.

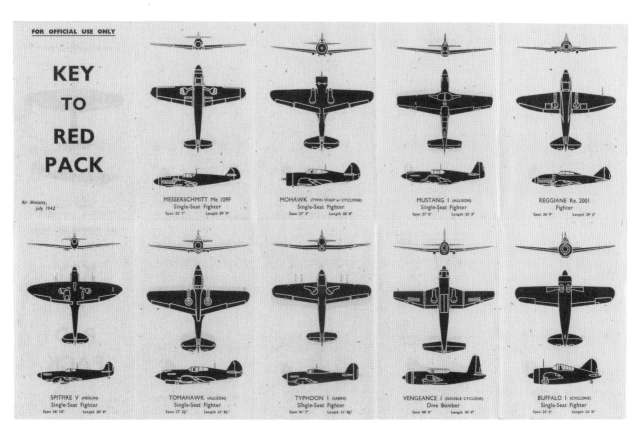

KEY
TO
RED
PACK

Air Ministry,
July 1942

MESSERSCHMITT Me 109F
Single-Seat Fighter
Span 32' 7"   Length 29' 9"

MOHAWK (TWIN WASP or CYCLONE)
Single-Seat Fighter
Span 37' 3"   Length 28' 8"

MUSTANG I (ALLISON)
Single-Seat Fighter
Span 37' 0"   Length 32' 3"

REGGIANE Re. 2001
Fighter
Span 36' 9"   Length 29' 3"

SPITFIRE V (MERLIN)
Single-Seat Fighter
Span 36' 10"   Length 30' 4"

TOMAHAWK (ALLISON)
Single-Seat Fighter
Span 37' 3½"   Length 31' 8½"

TYPHOON I (SABRE)
Single-Seat Fighter
Span 41' 7"   Length 31' 8½"

VENGEANCE I (DOUBLE CYCLONE)
Dive Bomber
Span 48' 0"   Length 40' 0"

BUFFALO I (CYCLONE)
Single-Seat Fighter
Span 35' 0"   Length 26' 0"

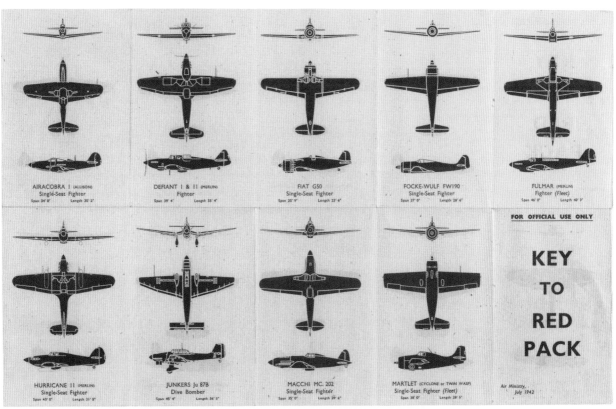

AIRACOBRA I (ALLISON)
Single-Seat Fighter
Span 34' 0"   Length 30' 2"

DEFIANT I & II (MERLIN)
Fighter
Span 39' 4"   Length 35' 4"

FIAT G50
Single-Seat Fighter
Span 35' 9"   Length 25' 6"

FOCKE-WULF FW190
Single-Seat Fighter
Span 37' 0"   Length 28' 6"

FULMAR (MERLIN)
Fighter (Fleet)
Span 46' 0"   Length 40' 3"

HURRICANE II (MERLIN)
Single-Seat Fighter
Span 40' 0"   Length 31' 5"

JUNKERS Ju 87B
Dive Bomber
Span 45' 4"   Length 36' 5"

MACCHI MC. 202
Single-Seat Fighter
Span 35' 0"   Length 29' 4"

MARTLET (CYCLONE or TWIN WASP)
Single-Seat Fighter (Fleet)
Span 38' 0"   Length 28' 5"

KEY
TO
RED
PACK

Air Ministry,
July 1942

CHARLES AND RAY EAMES

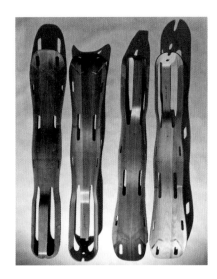

When Charles and Ray Eames (1907–1978 and 1912–1988, respectively), newly married, moved into a rented apartment in Los Angeles in 1941, they converted the spare room into a workshop where they built a plywood-moulding machine that they called, 'Kazam!', because it moulded the plywood like magic. The first design they manufactured was a splint **above**, based on a mould of Charles's leg and a year later the US Navy placed an order for 5,000 of them. The splint was also used to create the sculpture in their Christmas card for 1944 **right**.

In the years after 1945, the Eameses created some of the twentieth century's most lasting designs. Their iconic chairs built on the ideas of the Finnish architect, Alvar Aalto, who had worked in two-dimensionally bent plywood in the 1930s. Their designs were made possible by wartime advances in adhesives and the use of plywood to create three-dimensional curves in aeroplane fuselages.

The LCW (Lounge Chair Wood, 1946) **opposite** was the great breakthrough in their quest to provide affordable, comfortable furniture that could be easily mass produced. Where previously Charles had tried to create a seat and backrest in a single shell, he and Ray now created two separate pieces, joined by a plywood lumbar support, with plywood legs and rubber shock mounts that allowed the back to flex. The LCM (Lounge Chair Metal, 1946) **near right** with matching table, substitutes metal in the lumbar support and base, with self-levelling nylon glides. In 1956, the Lounge (670) and Ottoman (671) **far right** achieved a new level of comfort.

Behind their technical ingenuity and love of form is a playful *joie de vivre* which the Eameses applied to designs for ingenious children's toys, films, architecture and puzzles.

THE DETAILS ARE DETAILS. THEY MAKE THE PRODUCT. THE CONNECTIONS, THE CONNECTIONS, THE CONNECTIONS. IT WILL IN THE END BE THESE DETAILS THAT GIVE THE PRODUCT ITS LIFE. – CHARLES EAMES

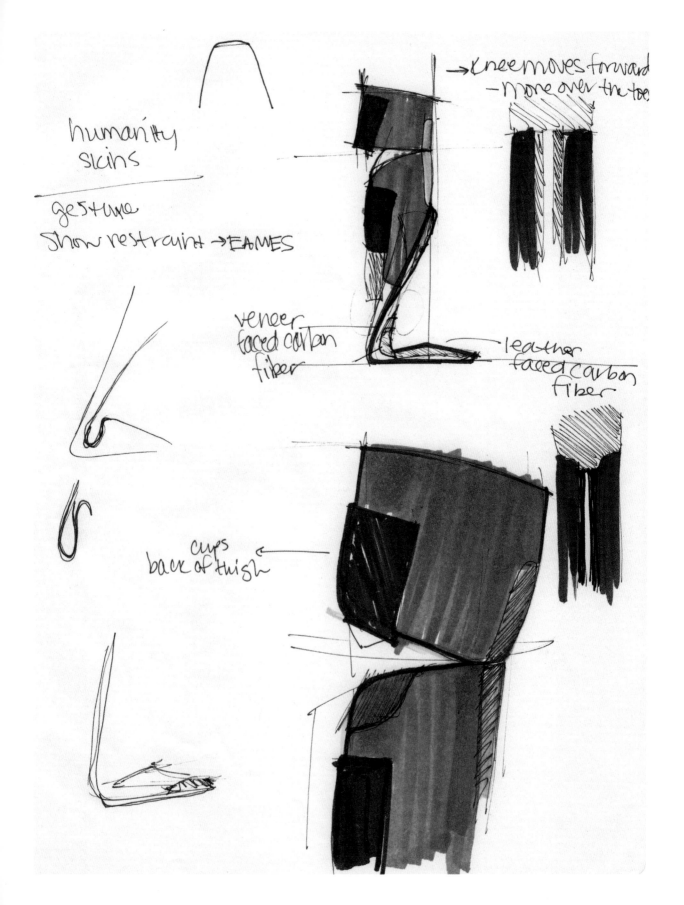

humanity
skins

gesture
show restraint →EAMES

veneer
faced carbon
fiber

knee moves forward
— more over the toe

leather
faced carbon
fiber

cups
back of thigh

134

The Eameses' use of moulded plywood has been one of the most influential innovations of the past 60 years. This design for a prosthetic leg (2007) **left** by Carnegie Mellon student Joanna Hawley employs rapid prototyping but the curved forms developed by Eames were hugely influential. 'Prosthetics generally lack humanity, style and grace. Often, they look much like landing gear and make the wearer uncomfortable, self aware and sometimes depressed,' writes Hawley. By referencing the Eames's use of materials and commitment to elegance and style, she and Kayhan Haj-Ali-Ahmadi, a medical student, 'designed a leg with Steve McQueen in mind. We sought to convey a creative use of positive and negative space, a balance of materials and a reflection of the wearer.'

Throughout their careers, Charles and Ray Eames worked closely with the American furniture manufacturer, Herman Miller. In 2007, the company commissioned 11 designers to reinterpret the classic Eames LCW, the results of which were auctioned at the Herman Miller Design Center to raise money for the Peace House Foundation. The designers included David Rockwell, Todd Oldham and Paula Scher, whose Pincushion chair **right** is a development of her Pincushion typeface. 'We wanted to think of the object as something soft that could be punctured, in this case, with large hatpins,' she said. 'In our expression, the chair becomes a purely visual, rather than a utilitarian object.'

Included was a design for a side chair with separate back and seat shells made of moulded walnut, ash, or birch plywood, with steel-rod frame legs and rubber shock mounts – which allowed the back to flex – joining the wood to the metal. This exhibited a stylish simplicity that was the result of many experiments to get the shape of the shells right. It still looks modern today. Writing about it in 1973, Arthur Drexler, the then Director of the Design Collection at the Museum of Modern Art, explained that, 'The distinctive and memorable image contributed by what is now called simply "the Eames chair" does indeed have about it something that seems American. It does not suppress necessary mechanical details but rather makes them plainly visible.'

Eames continued to experiment with moulded plywood until the mid 1950s. A folding screen was created in 1946, but his other classic was designed a decade later. This was a moulded plywood lounge chair and ottoman reputedly made for the film director Billy Wilder, which consisted of three rosewood shells, covered with leather cushions padded with foam and feathers (page 132). The chair was positioned on a five-pronged base made of polished black aluminium and became one of the most iconic chairs of the twentieth century.

New metals for old

Metals were also in demand during the war. Steel and aluminium were needed for aeroplane production and many civilian objects made from those materials were re-deployed to that end. In the aftermath of their wartime use, designers began to use metals in a new way.

The shortage of aluminium in wartime Britain led to the Aviation minister Lord Beaverbrook launching a campaign in 1940 – dubbed 'Saucepans to Spitfires' – to get people to donate their household aluminium goods to the war effort. At the end of the war the slogan was reversed because spare aluminium became available as a wood substitute for use in areas such as furniture manufacture. Ernest Race's little BA side chair benefited from the 'Spitfires to Saucepans' campaign that was promoted at the post-war 'Britain Can Make It' exhibition where a handful of designs – among them a Wells Coates-designed spaceship, an F.H.K. Henrion-designed aluminium-bodied sewing machine, a streamlined bicycle and an air-conditioned bed – were offered to whet the appetite of a nation hungry for new products.

At the end of the war, Race, who had been in the auxiliary fire service, set up his furniture company. He set about utilising scrap aluminium and ex-RAF upholstery fabrics: his BA chair, which had thin, splayed, extruded aluminium legs tapering to an elegant small ball foot, was made from re-smelted alloy. Race went on to create some of the iconic seating designs displayed at the 1951 Festival of Britain.

A car for the people

Car design was also affected by the war, and in Germany state control of design served one of Hitler's desired social aims – producing a car for the masses. Although the earliest version of the Volkswagen Beetle was not conceived by the state, but rather by the car engineer/designer, Ferdinand Porsche, Hitler backed it, seeing a role for it in his ambition to make Germany mobile.

In 1931 Porsche established an automotive consultancy in Stuttgart. A year later, with the NSU company, with bodywork made by Ruetter coachworks, and with the assistance of the car body stylist Erwin Komenda he created a prototype for what he called his 'Kleinauto Type 32', based on earlier work he had undertaken on the development of a small car for the masses. The car was rounded at the front and rear and the front door opened from a central hinge. It provided the base-line for the Volkswagen that was to take considerably longer to develop. (However, it was also remarkably similar to the T97 that Hans Ledwinka had produced for the Czech car-maker Tatra, and Tatra sued Porsche after the Volkswagen appeared. Hitler helped make the lawsuit disappear by invading Czechoslovakia in 1938, but in 1961 Volkswagen finally paid Tatra three million deutschmarks to settle the matter.)

Hitler came to power in 1933 and by the following year he had become aware of Porsche's experiments and commissioned some prototypes for a 'people's car' (Volkswagen). From that point the design of the car followed the parameters that Hitler laid down – the new car should not cost more than 1,000 Reichsmarks; it should be air-cooled; it should have a top speed of 62 miles per hour; and a fuel consumption of seven litres per 62 miles. It also had to be big enough to hold two adults and three children. The 'Type 60', as the new model was called, was tested by the Nazis which involved being driven 500 miles every day. A 1937 model introduced a split rear window and came to be known as the 'pretzel'. That year Hitler decided that the project should be state-funded and the Society for the Development of the German Volkswagen was formed.

The next stage of the project involved the creation of a factory that was opened in 1939. A town was selected and renamed KdF town (after Kraft durch Freude – Strength through Joy). Workers' housing and other facilities were also built as part of Hitler's new vision of town planning. However the advent of war stopped production of the car and the few cars that were produced during the war (around 200) were allocated to

Nazi chiefs. Following the war the British resumed production of the car and, on the factory being returned to German hands, the plant was restructured and renamed 'Wolfsburg'. Porsche's design proved to be highly successful and popular – truly a people's car; the designer himself was imprisoned for almost twenty months for his collaboration with the Nazis.

Utility on wheels
Another vehicle designed during the war also appealed in peacetime, though unlike the Beetle, the Jeep started out as a military object. The need for a fast, lightweight vehicle that could travel over rough ground had been apparent since the

The Eameses' moulded plywood chairs were also influential in the United Kingdom in the 1950s, as evidenced by the work of Robin Day and Ernest Race among others. Race's little Antelope chair combined a moulded plywood seat with a highly expressive steel rod frame and four little balls on the ends of the legs. It was one of the chairs that he created for outside use at London's Festival of Britain, held on the south bank of the Thames in 1951. A few years earlier Race had created his BA chair that had addressed the challenge of the unavailability of wood by using aluminium instead.

First World War but it wasn't until 1940 that the American government put out a call to manufacturers to design them something appropriate. The Bantam Car Company responded first and got to prototype stage, but the contract eventually went to Willys-Overland which worked with Ford to provide the US Military with what came to be called the Jeep. The vehicles were used for all kinds of war work, including transporting the wounded and acting as taxis.

In 1945 the first civilian Jeep went into production, marketed as a work vehicle for farmers. Ironically its functional, down-to-earth, utilitarian appearance helped transform it into an iconic object, valued for the way in which it had no pretensions to be anything other than what it was. In the spirit of the modernists – who had celebrated the aesthetically unselfconscious products of industry – products such as the Jeep were seen as highly desirable and were even raised to the status of 'cult' objects.

In 1951 the Jeep was selected as one of eight automobiles included in an exhibition at New York's Museum of Modern Art. It was described by the curator as 'a sturdy sardine can on wheels'. In 1946 American industrial designer Brooks Stevens created a Jeep station wagon – the Wagoneer. In 1974 he designed the Cherokee, the first sports utility vehicle, which owed much to the Jeep.

The story of the British Land Rover parallels, and indeed depends upon that of the American Jeep, and its design had the same no-frills popular appeal. Maurice Wilks, the chief designer at Rover at the end of the war, wanted to create a utility car for agricultural use. Because of steel shortages the car he designed in 1947 was made from aluminium alloy. In 1970 a more overtly styled version, the Range Rover, designed by David Bache, was developed to cope with tough terrain while also having strong visual appeal.

Wartime technology in the post-war world

The advances made in materials technology during the Second World War led to innumerable product innovations after 1945. In his book, *American Plastic*, Jeffrey Meikle lists many of the plastic products that were designed for the armed forces: 'They ranged from combs and razors, through molded bayonet handles, binocular cases, and mortar shell fuses, to resinous linings for jerry cans and stiffeners for fabric skins of carrier-based airplanes.' Nylon, which had been discovered in the 1930s by DuPont, had a variety of wartime applications including making parachutes.

Some post-war products owed their existence to the exigencies of war, whereas others were products that had been useful in wartime and could be re-designed to excite the expanded consumer market of the immediate post-war years. In Japan, for example Masaru Ibuka, who had run a firm called Japan Precision Instruments during the war, and Akio Morita, a young Navy lieutenant at the time, founded the Sony Corporation, immediately after the war. The firm's breakthrough came when the occupying American troops showed Ibuka a military tape recorder and, inspired by what he saw, he produced with Morita, the 'Type G', Japan's first tape recorder. It was a new phenomenon, and the Japanese public was not initially ready to buy it. Just as Josiah Wedgwood had had to market his utilitarian wares to persuade customers to buy them, so the duo set about marketing Ibuka's tape recorder intensively and educating potential consumers.

Wartime technology in the design of code-breaking machines related directly to the development of the object that now rules all of our lives – the computer. At Bletchley Park, Britain's code-breaking establishment in Buckinghamshire, the mathematician Alan Turing designed a number

The postwar success of the VW Beetle – and in particular its association with the 'flower power' movement of the 1960s and '70s – makes it almost incredible that its development was partly funded by the German National Socialists. German soldiers from an engineer battalion in Berlin-Spandau inspect an early version of the KdF (Kraft durch Freude, or Strength through Joy) Volkswagen in 1939 **left**.

Basic engineering and mass production meant that the Beetle was one of the first affordable cars of the 1950s, and it immediately became associated with a free and easy quality of life **right**. Its popularity quickly spread from Germany to the rest of Europe and the USA, and today it vies with the Toyota Corolla for the title of the world's best-ever selling car.

of electromechanical machines that used mathematical logic to analyse messages in the fiendishly difficult-to-break German Enigma code. After the war he joined the National Physical Laboratory, where he worked on the design of the ACE (Automatic Computing Engine) the first detailed design of a stored-program computer.

It was to help solve code-breaking mathematical problems that the the world's first programmable digital electronic computer, the Colossus, in operation from 1944, was designed. Because of wartime secrecy, progress in computing technology was not made generally known and many developments took place in different countries separately but simultaneously, the German Zuse Z3 and the US army's ENIAC machines among them. A lot more work has subsequently been undertaken, by engineers and designers, to get us to the point where we all have laptops on our desks, but the advances in programmability offered by Turing and the Colossus marked an important step forward.

New ways of living

Another influence of war upon design, perhaps as important as the development of new materials and technologies, was the new knowledge of how things could be done. The science of ergonomics – the study of the relationship between people and their environment, especially at work – advanced significantly in the Second World War. Work on human–machine interaction became increasingly important in finding the best way of using military equipment; for example it was discovered that better design of cockpit controls could eliminate common and deadly pilot errors. Although there was a sense that people on the battleground were ultimately expendable in the pursuit of winning the war, fitting machines to the sizes and capabilities of

their operators, and having effective control panels, were crucial to successful warfare. After the war this new knowledge fed back into a number of different areas. In Sweden, for example, it was rigorously applied to post-war buildings to house the expanding population. As space was at a premium it was important that minimum sizes were established, that storage was measured properly, and that beds and sofas were the right size. The Svenska Sjlödforeningen, later known as Svensk Form (Swedish Form), undertook scientific studies in the post-war period and developed sets of guidelines laying out the ideal sizes for objects destined for the domestic interior. In the US Henry Dreyfuss pursued a similar direction and invented a standardised human couple – Joe and Josephine – as the 'users' of a design that accounted for people's measurements and psychological needs.

The Second World War also impacted on the design of post-war housing in a number of ways. In Italy the physical devastation of war required an energetic building programme that resulted in the construction of blocks of flats in the suburbs of the main cities, Milan and Turin among them. In 1949 the Italian government generated a project, named INA-CASA, which aimed to significantly increase the amount of public housing in Italy. Several leading architect-designers of the day were involved, and polychrome ceramic plaques, designed by leading decorative artists, were fixed to all the buildings that were constructed.

Designing the world of tomorrow

Post-war Italian design combined the best of the past with that of the future. The relatively small size of the new Italian dwelling units challenged a new generation of architect-designers to create appropriate furniture items for them. Men such as Vico Magistretti, Carlo di Carli, Ettore Sottsass

Agricultural equipment surrounds a farmer's Jeep **left** in a 1945 demonstration of post-war uses for military vehicles.

The computer was one of the post-war products that owed at least part of its developments to wartime breakthroughs, for example in the design of code-breaking machines. The control panel of Olivetti's ELEA 7003 computer (1958/9) **right** was designed by Ettore Sottsass, who later went on to found the Memphis design group (pages 208–9). In the 1950s, a computer consisted of a number of discrete elements and filled a room. Sottsass's main contribution was to add colours to enhance user-friendliness and to alter the height of the cabinets so that operators could see one other.

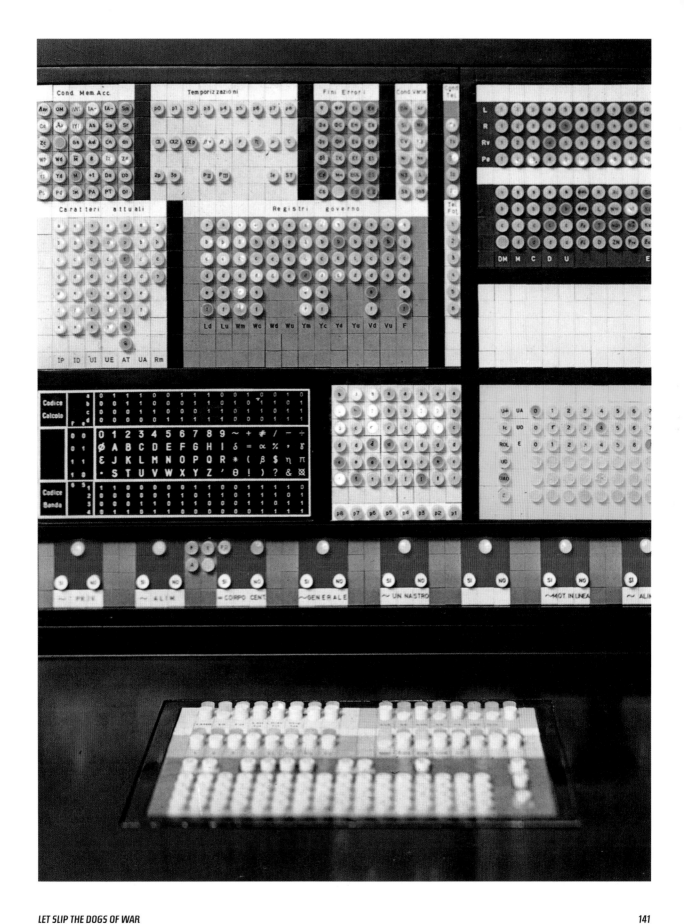

Marco Zanuso, and others, responded by creating lightweight, flexible, stackable chairs and other furniture items that both fitted into the new apartments and, through their simple appearance and use of new materials, contributed to the modern life-style. The first post-war Milan Triennale exhibition of 1947 showed several new furniture designs that were to be used in the new housing to a public hungry for such objects and ready to engage with the image of modernity. The enthusiasm of Italian manufacturers – Cassina, Artemide and others – to work with the architect-designers put Italy ahead of the game and set the foundations for a world-leading, post-war modern Italian design movement that reached a peak in the 1950s and 1960s.

Many countries hosted exhibitions immediately after the war to show the public the potential of design to enhance their lives and take them into the future. In 1946, for example, a large exhibition was organised by the National Research Council of Canada on the subject of Design and Industry, which sought to consolidate the advances that had been made during the war years. In Britain, the Council of Industrial Design, set up in 1944 to support high standards in the design of British products initiated an exhibition to open people's eyes to the importance of design. The result, 1946's Britain Can Make It, displayed pre-war goods for the most part, as industry had not yet had a chance to get back to production for peace, although there were a few streamlined modern designs. There was a strong emphasis on the role of the designer in the post-war context, however, and the Design Research Unit created a display – What Industrial Design Means – that charted the development of the design of an egg cup from the chicken through to the final product. Rather than putting down their pencils in wartime and waiting for the consumer economy to come

back into operation, designers were in huge demand during the Second World War and they grasped the opportunities it offered with both hands. In the process they both exploited and made possible a wide range of innovations – in the fields both of new technologies and materials – that influenced the forms and function of products. By 1951, the year of Britain's celebratory exhibition on the South Bank – the Festival of Britain – those innovations had all had an impact on a peacetime, civilian population and entered into the world of the consumer economy. The Festival's two important buildings – the Dome of Discovery and the Skylon – directly echoed the 1939 New York World's Fair's Perisphere and Trylon and expressed a similarly high level of technological utopianism about the world of tomorrow. With rationing nearly at an end, it was time to look forward to a prosperous future made possible by technology.

The years between 1939 and 1951 had seen a transformation of the modern world and, by 1951, the democratisation of material culture that had been promised in 1939 was beginning to become a reality. Above all else the war years had focused attention, urgently, on the basic needs of human existence and the importance of technological innovation. Design – in the hands of engineers, exhibition and graphic designers, furniture and fashion designers, architects, and ordinary people leading ordinary lives – had risen to the challenges presented to it. In the process the economic and psychological demands of the marketplace had been temporarily put to one side in favour of shared military, political and social goals. After the war there was an inevitable post-war swing back to a focus on individuals and their psychological needs. Design would meet these ever-growing needs in a post-war world filled with new looks, new material and new spaces.

The ninth Milan Trienniale in 1951 brought artistic responses of post-war experience to the fore. Luciano Fontana's *Spatial Light – Structure in Neon* **opposite**, was variously compared to a lasso, an arabesque and a piece of spaghetti. Fontana preferred to describe it as a, 'fantastical new piece of decoration' that enters into 'the aesthetic of the man on the street.'

The 1951 Festival of Britain was intended to mark the end of post-war austerity and the beginning of a new era that looked optimistically to the future and celebrated the contribution of designers to contemporary cultural life. The 90-metre/300-feet tall Skylon **left** perhaps refers in name and form to the Trylon at the New York World Fair of 1939 (page 112) and was designed by Hidalgo Moya, Philip Powell and Felix Samuely. Although popular with many people, *The Times* reported a joke that, like the British economy in 1952, 'it had no visible means of support.'

I DON'T THINK I EVER HAD SUCH A CLOSE RELATIONSHIP WITH A DIRECTOR AS I HAD WITH STANLEY KUBRICK. BUT HE WAS EXTREMELY COMPLICATED HIMSELF. AND IN TERMS OF DESIGN, HE QUESTIONED EVERY LINE I DREW, AND I FOUND THAT NERVE-DESTROYING, TO INTELLECTUALLY JUSTIFY MY LINES. IT BECAME LIKE A SESSION IN PSYCHOANALYSIS. – KEN ADAM

Not everything was rosy in the post-war world, and the spectre of a 'Cold War' loomed large in the collective consciousness. The depiction of the war room for Stanley Kubrick's *Dr Strangelove* (1964) **above** marks a prolific phase of creativity in the career of the German-born, British designer, Ken Adam, who also designed the film sets for many James Bond movies, including *Doctor No* (1962), *Goldfinger* (1964), and *Thunderball* (1965). Adam's design for the film set evoked a future Cold War world in which a mentally unstable US air force general orders a nuclear attack on the Soviet Union, and featured several thousand light bulbs. Steven Spielberg has called it the greatest set in cinema history.

THE CHAIR: PLYWOOD

From the 1930s up to the present, laminated plywood has inspired designers to create new and innovative chair forms. Paralleling the use of metals, especially tubular steel, as a structural material, bent, and later moulded, plywood was, however, both warmer and more responsive to the human body. Scandinavian designers, with their strong commitment to a humanistic approach to design, were especially drawn to it and their work – particularly that of the Finnish architect and designer Alvar Aalto – has acted as a stimulus to many others.

In the 1930s the English designer Gerald Summers, through his furniture production company Makers of Simple Furniture, pushed the design possibilities of bent plywood to the limits. His Lounge Chair (1934) **above** is made from a single sheet of plywood, cut and bent in two directions to create a seat, a backrest and two arms.

In the years following the Second World War, the expanded possibilities of plywood manufacture enabled the Danish Arne Jacobsen, following on the heels of Charles and Ray Eames (pages 132–3), to create his iconic Ant Chair **right**. It began life in 1951 as a three-legged chair, but by 1955 it had acquired four legs and its familiar anthropomorphic hour-glass shape. Compact, light and stackable, it quickly began to appear in modern interiors across the globe and continues to do so to this day.

In Japan the designer Sori Yanagi bridged the gap between east and west when he created his elegant Butterfly **opposite above** in 1954 from moulded plywood.

More recently another elegant design uses one length of plywood as innovatively as Summers did. The sinuous lines of Lorenzo Marassio's Plywood Fold Chair (2008) **opposite below** create the seat, backrest and legs in one continuous structure.

GUNS

The gun is the most totemic of all the 'killing machines', perhaps because of the relationship between weapon and user and because of its deadly efficiency. The British Sten submachine gun **top right** was one of the most ruthless – and basic – guns to come out of the Second World War. The Sten required minimal machining and manufacture, was cheap to produce and could be made in small workshops in just five man-hours – hence its Spartan appearance and very basic component parts.

A lot of Sten guns were airdropped to resistance fighters in Europe, such as the French partisan armed with a Mark II Sten in 1944 **above**. Outside of wartime, gun iconography is more ambivalent – not least in the US, where the right to bear arms is enshrined by the Second Amendment to the Constitution. Lieutenant Ellen Ripley in the *Alien* movies **opposite below left** and Lara Croft in the *Tomb Raider* games **opposite below right** carry their guns to quite different effect, Ripley being portrayed as a brave, almost degendered defender of mankind, Croft as a powerful woman whose sexual prowess is enhanced by her weaponry.

In Pyonyang, North Korea, artist Irina Kalashnikova photographed a massed audience holding up cards to create a huge image of a gun **opposite above**, surely a message to internal and external critics of the regime. Philippe Starck's Gun Collection for Flos (2005) **bottom right** – the Beretta bedside lamp, Kalashnikov AK 47 table lamp and M16 rifle floor lamp – provoked consternation in certain quarters when they were released. 'Why doesn't furniture show that everything is a political choice?' asked Starck. 'I am a designer and design is my only weapon so I use it to speak about what I think is important.' Twenty per cent of the revenue from sales of the Gun Collection is donated to the Italian human rights charity, *Fratelli del Uomo*.

www.tombraider.com

PREFABS

The ravages of war left many people without a home in the years after 1945. To fill that gap much effort was given to the design of prefabricated homes which could be produced and assembled easily and cheaply. In Britain the post-war 'prefab' was the result of a Temporary Housing Programme, established in 1944, that aimed to provide immediate housing for people whose homes had been destroyed in the war. The Ministry of Works took over responsibility for the design of prefabs which were given two bedrooms, a fitted kitchen, hot water and electric lighting. Different models were available, among them the Arcon Mark V, built round a tubular steel frame; the Aluminium Bungalow, which arrived ready-made on lorries and was designed by aircraft workers; and the timber-framed Phoenix. These prefabricated homes represented a vast life-style improvement for many people who were re-housed from bombed-out buildings. This image shows ex-serviceman Leonard Hickman looking at a Churchill all-steel with his family in 1944.

The design concept shown **opposite top** is a store for Puma made from prefabricated shipping containers and designed by LOT-EK. Using discarded materials, it consists of 24 shipping containers that can be taken apart and moved to new locations as necessary. The prefab **opposite** is a summer home designed by the Danish architect Henning Larsen on Vejby Strand.

LEGACIES

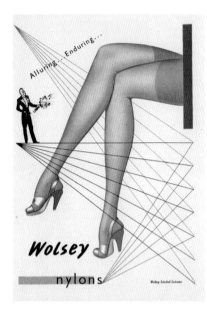

Without the material, technological and distributional advances that took place during the Second World War many now-familiar objects might be absent from our lives.

Nylon, invented in 1938, was developed during the war for uses such as making parachutes. In the post-war years, it was presented as a 'modern miracle', and nylon stockings **above** became part of popular American consumer culture. Similarly, after the development of mass manufacture of condoms **bottom right** in the 1930s, their ubiquity in post-war years was helped by the vast quantities issued to soldiers during wartime.

The ballpoint pen **top right** was invented by the Hungarian László Biró, in the 1930s. In 1943, he took out a patent, which was licensed by the British. Soon, ballpoint pens were being used in great numbers by the Royal Air Force, whose airmen found that the new pen worked much better at high altitudes than a fountain pen.

Ray-Ban Aviator shades **middle right** owe their iconic status to the US Army Air Corps, which adopted Ray-Bans when they were patented in 1937. When General MacArthur, Ray-Bans on his nose, landed in the Philippines during the Second World War, Ray-Bans acquired cult status, since assisted by movie stars like Tom Cruise.

The English Routemaster bus, designed by Douglas Scott in the mid 1950s, has been described as a 'Halifax bomber on wheels' as it owed so much to materials and techniques developed in aircraft production during the war. This prototype RM1 bus **opposite** is from 1956.

FOOLS OF FORTUNE

DESIGNING PLASTICS

The power of design had won battles and captured hearts and minds. Now in the years between 1945 and 1980 the nations of the industrialised world integrated design into their war-to-peace programmes, and used it to stimulate new markets and to create new identities for themselves. Through the late 1940s and 1950s designing for the market returned with renewed vigour, and the black-and-white era of the Second World War gave way to a brightly coloured world that attracted the eyes of post-war consumers. The thrill that had accompanied the purchase of a 1930s streamlined Hoover vacuum cleaner, with its brown bakelite body housing and black dust bag, for example, was lukewarm compared to the joy that came with the new ownership of a pastel blue, spherical 'Constellation' model from the 1950s, or the bright red, sculptural cleaner created by the Italian designer, Achille Castiglioni, from the same decade.

The new consumers looked to the glamorous, technology-led future that had been promised to an American audience at the 1939 New York World's Fair. In this they were encouraged by the advertising that bombarded them in their homes, in the pages of magazines and on the screens of their newly purchased television sets. In spite of the horrors of the atom bomb, and the anxieties caused by the Cold War which dominated the politics of the early post-war era, for most people living in the western, industrialised world, the 1950s and 1960s were optimistic, forward-looking decades of material affluence, made possible by design.

The optimism of life in those decades was accompanied by a 'throw-away' approach to material goods, a short-term relationship between people and their possessions. There was a price to pay for that of course. The low cost of oil at that time encouraged an extravagant, often profligate, use of that valuable resource – a resource that was essential to the production of plastics and to the expansion of car culture. Everyone began to feel that she or he was entitled to a nice, comfortable home and car, to fashionable clothes and other life-style accessories, to leisure activities, exotic foreign holidays and, most importantly, to self-expression through the acquisition of material goods. Increasingly these expectations became the norm, although inevitably, when the oil crisis of the early 1970s finally hit, they were to become luxuries that not everyone could afford.

The colourful, fairy-tale world of the 1950s, in which everyone felt like Cinderella with her new clothes and her car for a coach, owed much to the impact of the new materials – especially plastics – which flooded into the everyday environment making it possible for more people to invite countless new items, from pastel-coloured polyethylene food containers to patterned plastic laminate kitchen counters into their lives. Plastics also revolutionised the mundane world, however, through their transformation into furniture items and everyday household goods – buckets, washing up bowls and watering cans among them; into car interiors; into clothing and household fabrics; and as components in a multitude of other everyday objects.

Art and design can both seek to present the familiar in a new way. The artist Slinkachu photographs little model people that he poses in various situations around London streets. In *The Last Kiss* (2008) **previous pages** a couple share a romantic moment against the backdrop of the Embankment.

Without the advent of plastics the world of children's play would have been the poorer – or at least less colourful. In the 1960's and '70s, plastic toys became ubiquitous, **opposite**, although the low costs of materials and manufacturing sometimes meant that little attention was paid to 'good' design. The British Tri-ang company paid attention to and invested in the design of their Scalextric racing cars **top left**, but for every branded, design-led toy there were many generic examples, such as the plastic doll with cloth body **top right** and walking robot **bottom left**. Sometimes generic design cannot be improved upon – beach holidays would not be the same without a bright, plastic bucket and spade or an inflatable beach ball **bottom right**.

Synthetic materials – plastics in particular – took on new significant roles in these years. We'll look at where plastics came from and how design transfigured them in the post-war era. Their story is marked by recurrent waves of hot and cold feelings about them. At one moment people waxed lyrical about their new, miraculous properties, while at others they expressed deep anxieties about the vast quantities of synthetic materials that were invading the modern world, threatening the quality of life in the process and making it all too easy to over-consume.

As bakelite replaced celluloid, as acrylic and polyethylene replaced bakelite, and as the thermoplastic ABS and polyurethane foam came along in their wake, design gave plastics a purpose, but it was usually as imitators of natural elements rather than materials with their own messages. Designers tried to express or invent a distinct and distinguished identity for plastics, and seemed to be winning when cultural institutions, such as museums, granted a number of plastic products – for example the Tupperware food container – iconic status. However, they were ultimately defeated by the sheer quantities of goods made from these seductive, usually oil-based, man-made materials and by their impact everywhere in the world. Also taking over the world at the same time and bringing challenges and changes was another voracious consumer of oil – the car.

The stuff of dreams

The story of plastics starts in the middle years of the nineteenth century when the early 'natural' and semi-synthetic man-made materials, such as celluloid, casein, gutta-percha, vulcanite and shellac, were developed as substitutes for a range of luxury materials – including ivory, jet, amber, tortoiseshell and horn – which, in the second half of the nineteenth century, were in increasing demand by nouveau-riche Victorians but in diminishing supply. Celluloid, invented independently by the British Alexander Parkes and the American John Wesley Hyatt, was a magical material designed to provide the new market with goods ranging from jewellery, combs and knife handles to dolls and billiard balls. Technological advances brought bakelite, the first fully synthetic material, invented by Dr. Leo Baekeland of Yonkers, New York, in 1907; this dominated plastic's journey through the first half of the twentieth century. Like celluloid, bakelite was essentially a substitute material that spread the ownership of luxury goods even further. Promoted by popular magazines as a substance with miraculous properties and seen as an answer to dreams, the designer Paul T. Frankl explained in 1930 that, 'Base materials are transmuted into marvels of beauty.' Bakelite was available in dark brown or black, and, like celluloid, it too was soon challenged by yet more technological improvements as other plastics entered the marketplace offering products in a range of attractive colours.

The creation of a new dream world, in which goods were seen less as the products of factories than as magical objects that could have fallen out of the sky, was made possible by designers. It was they who created the streamlined bodies of radio sets, disguising their hitherto disparate elements in the process. Countless technologically complex objects were transformed into artefacts with strongly unified visual identities, whose workings were hidden from view. Brightly coloured radios, for example, graced furniture surfaces across the western world, Fada's little amber model being just one among many. Objects such as vacuum cleaners, which had previously presented enormous challenges to designers, now had

The Philco radio was one of the most modern objects in many 1930s British homes. It brought a taste of American streamlining, and the thrill of a new, modern material – plastic – into the lives of many British people for the first time. These women working on a 1930s factory line in Perivale, London, are involved in the manufacture of Philco radios. Their shiny, curved, Bakelite body-shells, which had been fabricated in moulds, disguise the complex workings that are contained within them.

unified plastic casings and could be seen as products with an individual identity. Working with plastics designers addressed the challenge of the enhanced competition arising in the inter-war years. Norman Bel Geddes's redesign of the Gestetner duplicating machine in 1929 was just one example of the countless dramatic product transformations that took place in the US. The replacement of its old-fashioned wooden case by a new, curvaceous bakelite body-shell magically transformed it from a boring office machine into a shining symbol of modernity.

Fabricated in moulds, plastic products had curved forms (which made it easier to extricate them from the moulds) and this nourished the craze for the streamlined style that became synonymous with the modern fashion. As a contemporary writer explained, 'modernistic trends have greatly boosted the use of plastics in building, furniture and decoration, and contrariwise, plastics by their beauty have boosted modernism.' This was not the craft-based modernism of the Bauhaus, rooted in the idealism of William Morris, however, but rather a new, commercially focused, market-led up-to-date vision conveyed by objects whose fabrication processes were unseen by their users and whose forms had little to do with their utilitarian functions but merely proclaimed their modernity.

Good design or bad

Immediately after the war years many designers were hugely optimistic about the potential of plastics to create a brave new world. The English writers, V.E. Yarsley and E.G. Couzens, captured that sense of euphoria in their account of the life of 'Plastic Man'. 'This creature of our imagination,' they wrote, 'will come into a world of colour and bright shining surfaces, where childish hands will find nothing to break, no sharp edges or corners to cut or graze, no crevices to harbour dirt or germs, because, being a child, his parents will see to it that he is surrounded on every side by this tough, safe, clean material which human thought has created.' 'Plastic Man' was to be enveloped by plastic items throughout his entire life, in his nursery, in his bathroom, when he travelled on a bus or on a train, at home and at school, when he played sport, in his office, when, as he aged, he needed false teeth and, when he finally died, in his coffin.

Others were more cautious about the way designers should work with plastics, adamant that they should have an intimate knowledge of their physical properties and capabilities; plastics had different forms, and this should motivate the designer at the outset. John Gloag, for example, explained that laminated plastics, 'may be plain or colour, with smooth, hard, glass-like polished surfaces; or a satin finish or texture may be imparted to the surface from patterns stamped on the metal sheets of the press wherein the sheets are formed,' and that the 'industrial designer will know how to handle such opportunities.'

In countries where plastics were suddenly available after being confined to the war effort, there was immediate enthusiasm for them. But, as the numbers of plastic products grew, and quantity inevitably took over from quality, they began to earn a reputation for being 'cheap and nasty'. Ironically, their very popularity began to backfire on them. In the US plastics had been introduced as substitutes for other goods and it had been the cheaper, lower-quality plastic products that had entered the civilian marketplace. Doubts began to emerge about the materials' relationship with good design; consumers began to be anxious that they were being sold 'vulgar' or tasteless goods, and disenchantment set in.

In Britain that strong sense of disenchantment was aggravated by the association of plastics with American popular culture. Members of the Council of Industrial Design, formed in 1944, were among those who became increasingly concerned about the presence of American commercial values on British soil and in 1952 Alec Davis, the editor of the Council's mouthpiece, *Design* magazine, sniffily declared that, 'American mass-production methods are hardly appropriate to the makers of, say, Staffordshire bone china, Yorkshire woollen cloth, Walsall leather goods, or London-tailored men's wear.' In that class-conscious country memories of quality, hand-made goods still ran deep and many people were suspicious of the brash new goods, as well as the items of poular culture – the films from Hollywood and the pulp novels – that were being imported from across the Atlantic. In the years before mass culture was taken seriously or even accepted, these imports were seen as a threat to traditional British values. Less parochially, Paul Reilly, subsequently Director of the Council of Industrial Design, was especially anxious about the malign effect on design arising from the sheer scale of the manufacture of plastic products: 'The temptation' he wrote, 'to adorn a moulding, to imitate carving or to impress a stylistic cliché, such as the 3 parallel lines, is certainly hard to resist when one considers the extreme reproduction of plastics.' It was an anxiety that was shared in Germany and France and which, in Italy, inspired modern architect-designers, from Roberto Menghi to Vico Magistretti, to establish a campaign to align plastic products with high culture by seeing them as objects of art.

Views like those of Paul Reilly encouraged a number of British designers to rise to the challenge of applying the Arts & Crafts principle of 'truth to materials' and 'form follows function' to plastic products. Paul Reilly tried to help, suggesting that plastics were viscous materials, and that the fact that they flowed into moulds should determine the forms of the products that were made from them. What he described as plastics' 'dead quality' should, he felt, be mitigated by a strong emphasis upon lively colour and flowing form. The results of the designers' efforts included some elegant pieces that have lasted the test of time, among them Ronald E. Brookes' 'Fiesta' range of crockery for Brookes and Adams of 1961, Gaby Schreiber's stylish objects, mostly kitchenware, for Runcolite, and David Harman Powell's stackable cups. They were all brave attempts to bridge the gap between craft manufacture and mass production and they have remained collectable 'classic plastics' to this day.

Plastic and parties

The simple and functional design of the polyethylene food containers made in the 1950s by the American Tupperware company was not, unlike Britain's 'classic plastics', deliberately stylish. Tupperware played an important role, nonetheless, in the American public's growing acceptance of plastics, while also helping to create a new market for plastic products. In spite of its straightforward appearance, or perhaps because of it, by the mid 1950s the Tupperware food container had been raised to the level of a high cultural icon and exhibited at New York's Museum of Modern Art, the home of 'good design'.

The story of these humble polyethylene containers is surprisingly rich. It illustrates how a non-styled product became a design icon, and demonstrates how a product can be branded by the marketing campaign that supports it. It serves as a reminder of the role gender plays in material culture, as well as how some products can straddle the worlds of high and popular culture.

The iconic livery of Allen Lane's Penguin paperbacks – orange for fiction, green for crime, blue for biography – was first seen in 1935, but in the postwar years became a formidable brand. *Lady Chatterley's Lover* was published in Britain in 1960 by Penguin Books, who were prosecuted under the 1959 Obscene Publications Act. The trial became a public event and a test of the new obscenity law. On 2 November 1960, the jury returned a verdict of 'not guilty', resulting in a far greater degree of freedom for publishing explicit material in the UK. The prosecution was ridiculed for being out of touch with changing social norms when the chief prosecutor, Mervyn Griffith-Jones, asked if it were the kind of book, 'you would wish your wife or servants to read.' The Penguin second edition, published in 1961, contains a publisher's dedication, 'For having published this book, Penguin Books were prosecuted under the Obscene Publications Act, 1959 at the Old Bailey in London from 20 October to 2 November, 1960. This edition is therefore dedicated to the twelve jurors, three women and nine men, who returned a verdict of "Not Guilty" and thus made D. H. Lawrence's last novel available for the first time to the public in the United Kingdom.'

EARL TUPPER AND BROWNIE WISE

Tupperware made its first appearance in 1946, developed by Earl Tupper (1907–1983) as an airtight plastic container for the kitchen. Two years later, he joined forces with Brownie Wise (1913–1992) and together **above** they created an innovative direct marketing strategy made famous by the Tupperware party. The Tupperware container made use of a new, translucent plastic material – polyethylene – that had been discovered in 1933 and used as an insulating material for radar cables during the Second World War. The containers were designed to store left-over food in refrigerators and they quickly became objects of desire for American suburban housewives.

In the early 1950s, Tupper and Wise embarked on direct marketing. Wise very cleverly realised that rather than selling Tupperware containers in retail outlets, where they looked unexciting, it would be much better to let women sell them to each other in their own homes. Thus was born the Tupperware Party, at which women bought the containers as gifts and combined buying things with creating social networks. The strategy proved enormously effective, as this party **opposite** from 1966 illustrates. Wise's ability to tap into popular culture, and the American dream of success, helped recruit thousands of women into a career at a time when a woman's role was conventionally tied to the home. Her noted TV appearances, magazine and newspaper articles made her a household name. In 1954 she became the first woman to appear on the cover of *Business Week*.

The patented 'burping seal' **above right** helped to distinguish Tupperware from its competitors. The use of colour was equally effective, as cheap and cheerful plastics became associated with bright, modern living. This 1962 'recruitment' advert **below right** emphasises the appeal of Tupperware's fashionable colours that matched other items in the home, as well as the potent combination of making money whilst socialising with friends and neighbours.

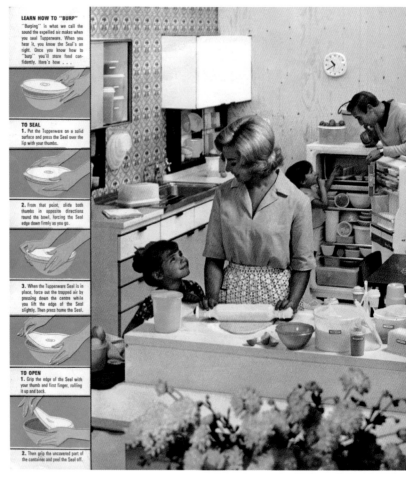

Have a Tupperware Home Party in April...

THE FRUITS OF LIFE FALL INTO THE HANDS OF THOSE WHO CLIMB THE TREE AND PICK THEM. – EARL TUPPER

From the 1960s onwards a wide range of plastics could be produced in bright colours that gave them instant eye-appeal. Plastics can be moulded into inventive forms, like these Eiko eggcups **above left**, designed by Christina Shafer and Alessi's little Cico eggcups, **below right**, which come complete with their own salt container and spoon, and combines the fun of bright plastics with the cartoon-like figurative nature of their imagery.

The plastic AnywayUp Cup **above right** was invented by Mandy Haberman and designed by Sebastian Conran and has a patented valve moulded into the mouthpiece to ensure that the spout seals between sips so that it does not spill when dropped or knocked over. The Tot cup with handles is designed for nine-month olds, whilst the Tumbler, behind it, is for slightly older toddlers.

In the early 1980s, the Swiss Swatch company responded to the decline in sales of traditional, luxury Swiss timepieces by introducing the Swatch **above**, using brightly coloured and decorative plastics in the manufacture of cheap, fashionable, fun watches that were extremely eye-catching and appealed to a wide audience. Swatches became both collectable and disposable, and in many ways they are a paradigm of the plastics conundrum – that here is a material that can be cheaply mass produced, but that needs to create a mass market that will buy and dispose on a regular basis because of the affordable price.

The red, upright, cordless electric kettle **left** is made by Bodum, a Danish company that is committed to making good-quality, well-designed plastic tableware and kitchenware.

Tupperware was invented in the US by Earl Silas Tupper, a former tree surgeon who moved into the plastics industry and set out to create an airtight food container. His aim was to ensure that left-over food could be stored in refrigerators thereby avoiding waste. The simple products he created were not intended for display, therefore, but rather to be stored away out of sight. As such they could not be sold on the basis of their appearance. Their most important selling point was, in fact, the seal joining the lids to the containers to make them airtight, a design feature that was only recognisable by the noise that was emitted when they were opened, dubbed the Tupperware 'burp'. The containers' near invisibility provided a serious selling challenge that was addressed, in the very early 1950s, by one of the company's door-to-door saleswomen, a single mother called Brownie Wise. Her strategy was to completely side-step the normal retail sector and to develop a concept of 'direct selling' that involved working face-to-face with female consumers in their own homes.

By the middle of the decade the 'Tupperware party' had emerged and countless suburban hostesses were using their homes for parties at which Tupperware items were sold. This subtle sales strategy built on the shift in emphasis, initiated in the pre-war years, from the housewife's identity as 'homemaker' and 'consumer' to her new one as 'hostess'. Brownie Wise 'Tupperised' suburban women by providing them with what they needed most (a social life rather than food containers), and by building on their desires. Tupperware items were bought first as gifts but gradually women felt able to purchase them for themselves. To offset the inherent rationality (waste-saving) of the Tupperware product, and to transform them into objects of desire, Wise introduced a high level of 'glamour' into the party

culture she promoted, setting the pace herself by wearing fashionable clothes, living with flamingo pink upholstery in her own home, and driving a pink Cadillac. Wise, in effect, designed an image and lifestyle for Tupperware, which is what women were buying when they bought these simple plastic goods.

In 1956, like the Jeep before it, the neutral Tupperware container was deemed to be an item of 'good design' by curators at New York's Museum of Modern Art. By that time it had come to be seen, in the words of Alison J. Clarke, as a 'shining beacon of hope in a period defined by an unprecedented rise in mass consumption and a perceived decline in mass consumer taste.' These unobtrusive, practical objects were seen to have reversed that trend and to have repositioned the designer-engineer, rather than the popular stylist, as the hero of the modern world. The Museum of Modern Art's validation of the Tupperware container however, ignored the fact that its success was due to its novel method of marketing rather than the inherent effectiveness of its simple design.

The quest for oneness
An earlier Museum of Modern Art project, the 'Low Cost Furniture Competition' of 1948, saw Charles Eames present what he called his DAR chair, essentially a moulded fibreglass shell mounted on to a metal frame. This was an important advance in one of the most compelling challenges that faced designers and manufacturers from the late 1940s through to the 1960s: the search for a one-piece plastic chair, an aesthetically desirable concept that, if achieved, could ultimately simplify the manufacturing process. The DAR chair was the first of its kind and was to inspire several other designs that followed in its wake, among them the English designer

in removing plastic objects from moulds, combined with the materials' limited structural strength, meant that a single-unit, all-plastic chair would have been impossible to produce.

With its seat ribbed for strength and its four sturdy legs, the child's stacking chair designed by the Milan-based designers Marco Zanuso and Richard Sapper was completely fabricated in plastic and also presented itself as if it had been manufactured as a single unit. Closer inspection reveals four seam lines near the top of the legs, however, joining them to the combined seat and back that was moulded in a single piece. The 4867 chair, designed by the Italian designer Joe Colombo for Kartell in 1968, was, like Zanuso and Sapper's child's chair, also a 'cheat' inasmuch as its four legs were made individually, and linked to its one-piece moulded seat and back shell. The shiny surfaces of this elegant chair, which was available in pillar-box red, white, apple green or black, helped direct the observer's eye away from the seam lines that are located halfway up the legs.

In spite of the numerous efforts that American and Italian designers made in this arena the prize for the design of the first one-piece plastic chair actually went to the Danish designer Verner Panton. Designed and prototyped in 1960, but not manufactured until a few years later, Panton's strikingly beautiful S chair, with its cantilevered seat and weighty base, addressed the idea of a single-piece plastic chair from quite a new direction and succeeded where others had failed.

It wasn't until 1980, however, that the mass-produced 'monobloc' plastic chair finally emerged. The first model was created by the French company, Grosfillex, but it was rapidly copied by manufacturers across the globe. The end of this design and manufacturing quest was not an unalloyed success, since this cheap, weather-proof, stackable plastic chair has become

Robin Day's hugely successful polypropylene stacking chair – another moulded shell mounted on metal legs – which was launched by Hille in 1963. Day's chair quickly became a ubiquitous object in a wide variety of public spaces, from school classrooms to church halls. Eames's colleague Eero Saarinen, also took up the challenge of exploiting plastics' properties in his Tulip chair design, which looked like a one-piece plastic chair but which actually consisted of a moulded plastic shell mounted on to a metal pedestal. Its all-white, flowing profile disguised the shift from one material to another, giving an illusion of a single unified form. The practicalities involved

Eero Saarinen's Tulip chair (1957) was among the first chairs to look as if it was made completely out of plastic. In fact its base is made of metal but it is artfully blended with the plastic seat to give an impression of material unity. In spite of this deceit it was a strikingly modern-looking chair when it appeared and it remains one of the twentieth century's most iconic designs. The bright red seat cushion is made from polyurethane foam, which first became commercially available in 1956.

a familiar sight, often damaged and frequently abandoned, in countless public spaces, causing both the design and the material to become severely devalued. Indeed a sense of cultural pessimism, or dystopia, accompanied the monobloc chair's ever deeper intervention into everyday life. The disenchantment with plastic that emerged was linked to its ubiquity but also to its lack of biodegradability. It brought to an end the earlier enthusiasm for plastics' potential to enhance the quality of life. While designers continue to use plastics in innovative ways to make striking statements, in general plastics continue to have a relatively poor reputation as they present themselves to the world.

Italian chic

The enthusiasm for plastic products that existed up to the 1970s had been largely the result of Italy's design contribution. A variety of factors made Italy a unique and fertile hotbed for the post-war modern design movement. They included the late emergence of Italy's programme of industrialisation, which retained a craft base within it, combined with the country's post-war desire to become a modern democracy of international significance. There was also a generation of architect-designers, who had trained as modernists in the inter-war years, but who had hitherto lacked the opportunity to work with industry. However, during the inter-war years Italy had developed its own celluloid industry and, led by the Nobel-winning chemist Giulio Natta, made significant progress in the research into, and manufacture of, other plastics as well. Immediately following the war, thanks largely to American Marshall Aid, the country began to develop its own plastics manufacturing industry and by the early 1960s the growth of Italian plastics production was second in the world after that of the USA.

As elsewhere, however, Italian consumers were unimpressed by the quality of the plastic products available to them in the 1950s, and emerging industrial designers focused on the improvement of plastic products as one of their main challenges. By the mid 1960s, supported by the Milan Triennale exhibitions and the powerful Italian design press – Domus, Ottagono and Stile Industriale among others – Italian designers had produced some of the most sophisticated and elegant plastic products in the world.

The Italian designer, Joe Colombo, went one step further than Saarinen in the creation of an all-plastic chair with his Universale stacking chair of 1965–7 **above left**, produced by Kartell. Although Colombo was the first to use injection-moulding in chair manufacture he was unsuccessful in his ambition to make the chair a single piece, as the joins at the top of the legs indicate. The chair, which came in bright red, green, black or white, was available in three different heights. The hole in the back, which was introduced to make it possible to get the chair out of the mould, also acted as a handle when it needed to be lifted.

Colombo's sketch for a small armchair with curved elements (1964) **right** represents a stage in his journey towards the all-plastic Universale. At this point, however, he was experimenting with the possibilities of bent plywood, just as many other designers had done before and have done since. He was particularly interested in the ways in which chair components fitted together and with the possibility of manufacturing chairs in efficient, simple ways.

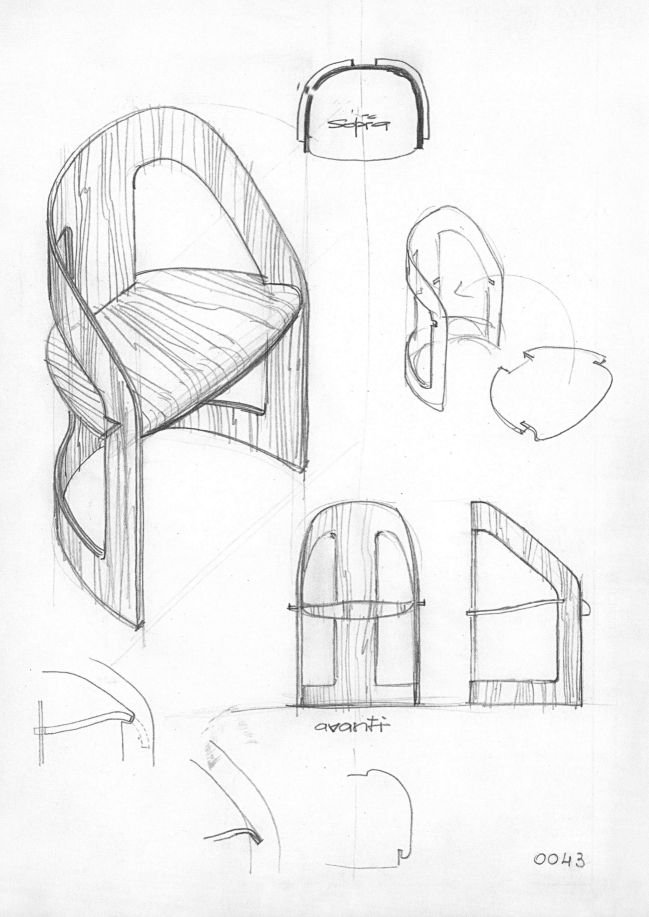

sopra

avanti

0043

VERNER PANTON

CHOOSING COLOURS SHOULD NOT BE A GAMBLE. IT SHOULD BE A CONSCIOUS DECISION. COLOURS HAVE A MEANING AND A FUNCTION. – VERNER PANTON

Verner Panton (1926–1998), pictured in 1969 with his wife, Marianne, and daughter, Carin, in his Living Tower (1968) **above** was one of Denmark's most innovative designers. Trained both as an architectural engineer and as an architect, he had a keen eye for materials and for the structural possibilities of furniture pieces. After an apprenticeship with Arne Jacobsen between 1950 and 1952 – which included some assistance developing the Ant chair (page 146) – Panton set out on his own. He liked working with bright coloured plastics and created a number of highly innovative chairs that ignored the traditional distinctions between elements – seats, backrests and legs. From the late 1960s, he experimented with the traditional divide between furniture objects and environments and his work became synonymous with progressive, 'counter-cultural' thinking .

The Heart Chair (1959) **bottom right** is the first, distinctive manifestation of a Panton style. It is a radical departure from the traditional furniture object, achieved by thinking of chairs as a single element rather than as a set of component parts. The drama lies in what looks like the precariousness of the bottom point of the heart balancing on a stainless steel base unit. A strong structure ensured that there was no danger to the sitter, but the visual impact was dramatic. His wire Cone Chair (also 1959) **opposite** is a variation on the same themes. This time a wire frame and a curved back, combined with foam seat and back pads for comfort, offered a more open structure. There was the same precariousness, and a swivelling mechanism was included to give the sitter the possibility of movement.

The S Chair (1960) **top right** was the first single-form, injection-moulded plastic chair ever. By rejecting the idea of a chair having four legs, Panton created a radical solution to the sitting object, one that saw the back rest, seat and support as a single, flowing unit.

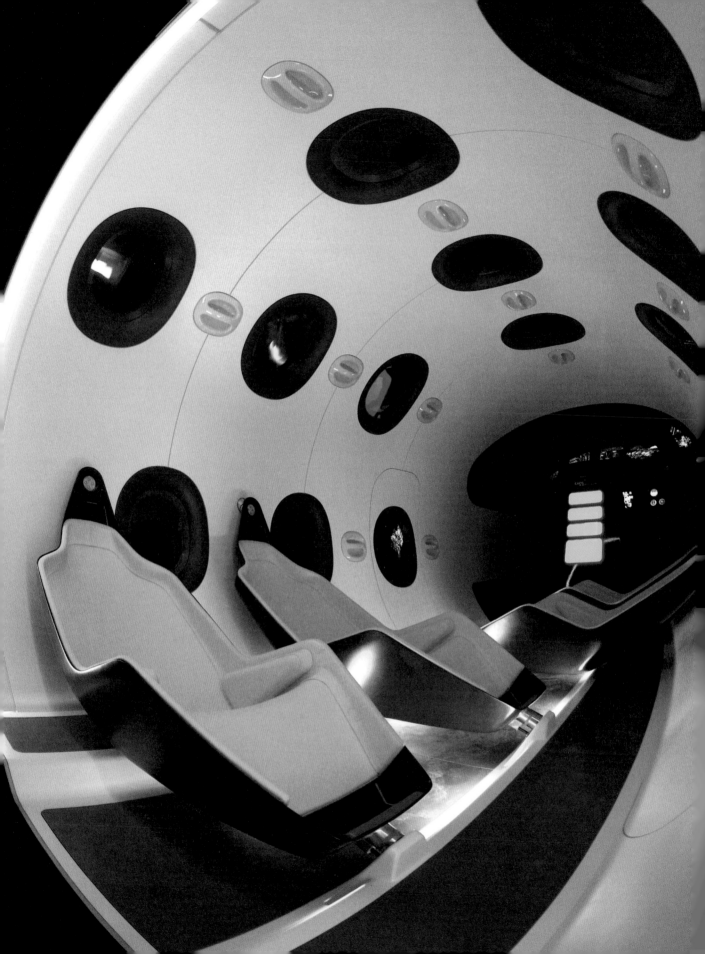

Taking informality to its limit, Panton's Phantasy Landscape, exhibited at the Furniture Fair, Cologne, in 1970, **previous pages** was made of wood and covered with colourful upholstery. It moved completely away from the idea of the individualised sitting object and embraced a much more environmental and communal definition of seating. This approach required a significant amount of physical flexibility on the part of its participants and was aimed at young people who were happy to lounge around and interact with others.

The idea of an integrated interior, championed by Sixties radicals such as Panton and Colombo, is particularly relevant to spaces in which every element needs to be controlled. The Australian product designer, Marc Newson, worked with EADS Astrium on the interior of their new space plane (2007) **left**, an interior in which weightlessness will occur. Newson's trademark

use of bright colours creates striking visual impact in his 1989 felt chairs for Cappellini **above**. Like Panton, Newson experiments with the chair's form: the hard surfaces and curvaceous forms of this chair's fibreglass shell are precariously supported at the back on a single polished aluminium leg, a feat of design engineering that is on a par with Panton's Cone chair (page 171).

Ron Arad's Big Easy armchair (1988) **left** is one of a series in which he experimented with the contrasts between weight and weightlessness. Made of sheet steel which has been beaten and welded by hand, this chair is less about comfort and more about the idea of a chair made of a material that stands at the other end of the spectrum from the comfortable, buttoned upholstery that is more usually found in a voluptuous armchair of this kind.

Panton's experiments in environment and form have echoes in Thomas Heatherwick's East Beach café in Littlehampton (2005) **top**, which is comprised of a pre-fabricated steel outer layer cut into vertical slices. The structure resembles that of a ship's hull and the steel will rust as it ages, melding the building with its seaside setting.

From Gino Columbini's bucket for Kartell – transformed by the photographer from Domus from a banal artefact to a quasi-art object – and his little lemon squeezer for the same company, to Marco Zanuso's innovative foam rubber armchairs for Arflex, Italian designers and manufacturers re-defined the plastic product as an ultra-elegant piece of 'good design', as important to the modern lifestyle as chic leather furniture and marble coffee tables. Also influential were a series of innovative plastic furniture pieces designed by Vico Magistretti for Artemide in the early 1960s, among them his famous, brightly coloured 'Selene' chair, originally made in ABS, which featured sleek shiny surfaces that were hard to the touch.

Designers also turned their attention to the creation of the plastic casings of electrical goods. Castiglioni's bright red REM vacuum cleaner of 1956, for instance, fulfilled Paul Reilly's heartfelt plea of a few years earlier for designers to focus on plastics' 'natural' qualities and their visual implications, namely fluid forms and bright colours. Ettore Sottsass's little Valentine typewriter, produced by Olivetti in 1967, was also a study in red plastic confirming the belief that the design of plastic products could follow the 'truth to materials' rule, even if that 'truth' arose from something that was artificially created rather than, as William Morris would have preferred it, derived directly from nature.

National style

The sophisticated metal and plastic body housings of the strikingly modern items of audio equipment and television sets that were produced in Italy, especially those by the Brionvega company, made them resemble pieces of abstract, organic sculpture and gave them a recognisable, specifically 'Italian' identity. Other countries were also producing goods with identifiably national characteristics. While Scandinavian countries depended largely upon their simple wooden furniture and their ranges of decorative art objects – glass, ceramics and metalwork in particular – Germany's electrical products exhibited hard-edged geometric forms. That country's highly rational, functionalist approach was especially visible in the plastic and metal housings of electrical goods produced by the Braun company. The designs that Dieter Rams created for Braun were characterised by sharp corners and straight, parallel sides which challenged the metal stamping and plastics moulding techniques that produced them. Braun first received international attention through the television sets and radios that it exhibited at the Düsseldorf Fair in 1955. In his search for a new, modernist aesthetic for electrical goods Rams found a solution that enabled plastics to enter the hallowed world of 'gute Form' (good form). The body shell of his 1957 'Kitchen Machine' food mixer, for example, brought metal and plastic together in the creation of a highly unified and rigorously geometric shape. It was later emulated by the English designer, Kenneth Grange, in his famous 'Chef' food mixer for Kenwood, although it was designed with the English market in mind and the lines were therefore a little softer.

Pop goes plastic

Plastics could be designed to form such a myriad of items – in any shape, any form, any colour – that their nature seemed chameleon-like. This meant that they could don the mantle of good design at one moment and reject it at another. And without plastics the pop design movement, which challenged and subverted such notions of good and bad, could not have produced some of its most lasting icons. Alongside the loud music,

The innovative hi-fi unit that the Italian architect-designers, Achille and Pier Giacomo Castiglioni designed for Brionvega in 1965 represent Italian product design at its most radical. Careful attention was paid to the positioning of the instrumentation and the control knobs while the form could be modified by lifting the speakers up on the deck when the machine was not in use. The Castiglionis rejected the traditional dark, wood-grain finish of conventional hi-fi sets, which made them like pieces of furniture rather than items of equipment, and utilised, instead, a light coloured plastic laminate to give it a modern look.

the colourful clothes and other 'fun' lifestyle accessories that characterised 1960s Britain – that centre of pop, or youth, culture – a number of plastic products also played a role in overturning what had up to that point looked like the universal values of 'good design'.

Pop design set in motion a wholesale rejection of the values of inter-war modernism which had insisted that an object's outer form should reflect its means of production. For pop design, objects need express nothing more than fashion. The fashion-conscious society that produced and consumed them was committed to short life-cycles and to the idea that it is better to throw away an object, once it has outlived its ability to express the moment, than to keep it. Pop design represented an acceptance, on the part of both designers and consumers, that design should be led by the needs of the marketplace rather than those of manufacturing. Real disposability – possible, for example, with paper clothing – was one way forward, but it was accompanied by other things that could not actually be thrown away but which resisted permanence by being able to change their forms and refresh themselves. Although disposability was, ironically, clearly a problem for plastic products, many of the newer plastics were inherently soft and flexible and ideally suited to the new culture of accelerated change.

The introduction of high-frequency welding used to join together pieces of vinyl chloride that has been polymerised with vinyl acetate resulted in a new version of PVC that was both tough and flexible. This in turn led to the creation of inflatable objects which became an important part of the material culture of pop. Combining transparency, softness, and flexibility this material provided a dramatic contrast to the hard, modernist ABS surfaces of Magistretti's

and Joe Colombo's chairs, and designers used it deliberately to oppose those images of monumentality and permanence. Inflatability became synonymous with the idea of impermanence which pop design liked so much, and with the idea of rooms, settings and objects that were temporary. The 1960s saw the English architectural group Archigram introducing flow and movement into their idealised urban designs, believing that 'chairs are on the way out and pneumatic seating, which forms to the body when sat on, will take its place.' The English architectural critic Reyner Banham proposed a plastic bubble as a new solution to the house, and the Italians, Scolari, De Pas, D'Urbino and Lomazzi, adherents of the Italian 'anti-design' movement (a radical anti-modernist group), produced an inflatable plastic chair for the Zanotta company. Several other versions of the same idea appeared in a number of different countries, including the 'Pumpadinc' armchair designed by the British Arthur Quarmby, and a fake-fur-covered version created by the record-cover illustrator Roger Dean, produced by Hille. The French designer Quasar Khanh, designed a number of inflatable PVC chairs and armchairs that could be filled with air, coloured gas or water. Not only was inflatable furniture here one minute and gone the next it also suggested a whole new way of living that eroded the distinction between indoors and outside – Zanotta's chair, for example, was as at home in the swimming pool as in the living room. Inflatable furniture also challenged the permanence of the built-in furnishings so beloved by the inter-war modernists.

Graphics and typography were also affected by the ethos of pop and they, in turn, also proposed ways of rejecting their own modernist roots. The simplicity and seriousness of early twentieth-century typography, for example, was challenged

by a use of playful cartoon imagery. From the psychedelic pop posters designed by Hapshash and the Coloured Coat and Martin Sharp in Britain and by Wes Wilson in California, to the almost undecipherable typefaces used in the page of *Oz* magazine, graphic design lost its hard edge and became absorbed into the fun world of pop.

PVC also found its way into fashion garments. The Parisian couturier, Courrèges, for example, used it to translate the imagery of science-fiction and space-travel into zany clothing items. The fashion writer, Meriel McCooey, described the material's inherent futurism: 'It's a material you can't work nostalgically,' she explained. The pages of mid 1960s fashion magazines were filled with images of PVC halter-neck dresses, space-shaped visors and models striking robotic poses. To accentuate their space-age effect Courrèges dressed his models in slitted white plastic glasses and white calf-high plastic boots.

Polyurethane foam was also hugely popular. Like PVC, it allowed a high level of flexibility to enter into furniture design. A number of Italian design groups used the soft forms made possible by designing with polyurethane in a deliberate challenge to the solidity and monumentality of that country's most successful neo-modernist creations. Archizoom's 1966 wave-shaped 'Superonda' sofa-bed, for example, exploited polyurethane foam's sculptural possibilities, while, in the following year, the sculptor, Piero Gilardi, produced 'Rocks'– lumps of foam resembling large pebbles but which gave way under the impact of someone sitting on them. Hard was replaced by soft, permanence by impermanence. Gruppo Strum created the extraordinary 'Big Meadow' – a 'furniture' piece consisting of great fat 'fingers' of green foam that you could sit or lie on – in the same year, while Gaetano Pesce's series of UP armchairs, designed

for C & B Italia, expanded as they were released from the flat-packs that enclosed them and held them down. Perhaps the most influential of the Italian pop chairs to exploit the properties of the soft plastics, however, was the 'Sacco' seat, designed by Piero Gatti, Cesare Paolini and Franco Teodoro, and produced by Zanotta in 1969. Filled with thousands of polyurethane pellets the seat had no fixed form of its own but changed its shape when its users sat upon it. It was the model for the ubiquitous beanbag that can still be found in many a teenager's bedroom. As with Gilardi's design this served to give the human body authority over the sitting object rather than the other way round as was the case with modernist – or indeed most – chair designs.

Ettore Sottsass's use of plastic laminate was an important component of that inspirational designer's critique of modernism. It helped him emphasise the surface of his objects and to minimise their three-dimensional solidity, to focus on image not form. For example Sottsass applied decorated plastic laminate to the surfaces of the wardrobes he created for Poltronova in 1966 in order to emphasise the flatness of their surfaces. The fact that plastics are chameleon materials that can be made to look very different in different contexts enabled Sottsass to reinforce his consistent message that form should not follow function. A small group of Finnish furniture designers also embraced the pop aesthetic in the 1960s and used plastics in provocative ways. Eero Aarnio and Esko Pajamies were both committed to moving the idea of the chair away from the conventional seat/back/four legs formula and to create innovative forms that could still, nonetheless, work as seating objects but in a much less formal way. Aarnio's Ball Chair – a hollow sphere on a slim stand with an opening for a seat – and the even more space-age Bubble

MacLean Bonnie's 1967 poster **left** is typical of the fin-de-siecle-inspired psychedelic graphics of the 1960s. The swirling peacock feathers and androgynous face are redolent of the work of members of the late nineteenth-century aesthetic movement – Aubrey Beardsley (page 67) in particular. Now collectable, such a poster was a throwaway design at the time.

The inflatable Blow chair **right**, designed by de Pas, D'Urbino and Lomazzi in 1967, was made of high-frequency electronically welded PVC, and fabricated in a range of colours by the Italian company, Zanotta: a Pop-inspired anti-chair that was as at home inside as it was outside.

Chair – a transparent hollow sphere suspended from above – are classic icons of modern design. The Danish designer, Verner Panton, also used plastics in a highly radical way in the 1960s in the furniture environments he created. By using the flowing shapes of plastics and the soft forms of some of them – polyurethane foam in particular – he challenged the ways in which people normally live in their houses. He ignored the idea of isolated furniture items, replacing them with a complete, whole plastic environment in which people could adopt a wide range of poses and sitting/lounging positions – ones that were completely different from those dictated by,

say, the upright armchair. This would also encourage new forms of human interaction in domestic spaces.

Cars for the people
From the 1950s onwards, plastics were increasingly being used in cars, moving from their instrument panels to their interiors in general, to becoming fully integrated into their bodywork. For example, the roof of the stylish, futuristic Citroën DS – a design sensation when it was unveiled at the 1955 Paris Motor Show – was made of unsaturated polyester reinforced with fibreglass, a combination that came to be used

Typography and graphic images became more cartoon-like and provocative in the 1960s and 1970s. *Oz* magazine was first published in Australia in 1963. When its founder Richard Neville moved to the UK, a British version was launched in 1967. *Oz* was a deliberately shocking, youth culture publication that pointed two fingers at the establishment and, to that end, it employed graphic artists such as Robert Crumb **above left** and Martin Sharp, whose psychedelic imagery and cartoon-like drawings created an appropriate visual language to match the provocative texts that it frequently contained. The notorious School Kids Issue (May 1970) **above right** invited secondary school children to edit the magazine. One 15-year-old pasted the head of Rupert Bear on to an explicit, 'X-rated' cartoon by Crumb, and the magazine was subsequently prosecuted under the Obscene Publications Act. According to the prosecutor, Mr Brian Leary, 'It dealt with homosexuality, lesbianism, sadism, perverted sexual practices and drug taking.'

Graphic designer Jamie Reid was part of Punk, a British anti-establishment youth culture of the lates 1970s that used lifestyle accessories – such as clothing, record covers and posters – to express its contempt of the status quo. Reid used letters cut from newspapers to resemble ransom notes, including one featuring the Queen's head with ransom-style writing covering her eyes and mouth **right** that was used as a promotional poster for the Sex Pistols' 1977 single, *God Save the Queen*.

fairly widely in car body parts. Britain's Ford Cortina, launched in 1962, had an all–plastic interior. More recently, the apparently simple idea of adding plastic cup holders on to the rear of the front seats of cars, pioneered by Renault's Megane Scenic of 1996, which was designed by a woman, Anne Asensio, came to be seen as a significant feature in car sales.

Cars were of course dependent, as was the production of plastics, upon oil which, in the immediate post-war years was relatively cheap and available. Car culture penetrated nearly all levels of society, bringing with it many new design opportunities, not just for the vehicles themselves but also for the new designs and environments that supported them, from petrol stations, motorways and their sign systems, to advertising campaigns. The concept of a 'people's car' became hugely popular, encouraging the public to give up their bicycles and motor-scooters and to embrace the affordable small car. Volkswagen's 'Beetle' entered mass production, while Italy's little Fiats 600 and 500, France's Citroën 2CV and Britain's Morris Minor and Mini were popular additions to Europe's roads.

Dante Giacosa, who had trained as an engineer, had created the first 500 model for Fiat, the 'Topolino', back in 1936. In the post-war years the demand for a small car to compete with the Vespa and Lambretta motor-scooters that buzzed around the narrow streets of Italy's cities became increasingly strong and the designer modified his earlier model in response, introducing four seats and reducing the sizes of the bonnet and the boot to give his little rear-engined car an integrated appearance. The 600 proved an overnight success and Giacosa went on to design the new 500 which was even smaller. Its sloping back gave it a more rakish appearance than the 600 and new engineering gave it more acceleration. It remained in production until 1975 and proved extremely popular. It has recently been revived in a modified form to suit the needs of the early twenty-first century.

The first mass-produced version of France's people's car, the Citroën 2CV, came off the production line in 1948. A pilot in the First World War, Pierre Boulanger, the little car's designer, had worked closely with its engineer, Henri Lefèvre, an expert in aircraft technology, and its stylists Flaminio Bertoni (an Italian who worked both as a sculptor and as a car stylist) and Jean Muraret, back in the 1930s. The original model had been developed for French farmers and, famously, had to be able to transport four people, or two farmers and a large bag of potatoes, across a field without breaking the eggs they carried with them in a basket. A prototype was produced in 1936 and 250 models were manufactured in 1939. The car depended upon a lightweight magnesium alloy chassis; its structural members were perforated for additional lightness; and corrugated metal was used for strength in emulation of the Junkers airplane. Mica was used for the windows and cloth and tubular steel for the seats. The 1939 prototype provided the basis for the post-war version which was launched at the 1949 Paris Automobile Salon. 'The four wheels under an umbrella,' as Boulanger described the car, remained virtually unchanged, with only minimal modifications, right up to 1990 when production of it finally ceased.

Britain's two people's cars – the Morris Minor of 1948 and the Austin/Morris Mini produced eleven years later – were both the creations of the engineer Alec Issigonis. Like Giacosa he approached the discipline of car design with the whole car in mind rather than focusing merely on the form and decoration of its body as the American car stylists tended to do.

DIETER RAMS

The German industrial designer, Dieter Rams (b.1932) **above** is associated more than any other person with the rational machine aesthetic that characterised German products of the post-1945 era. Many of his designs were realised by the Braun company that first employed him in 1955 and for which he was chief designer between 1961 and 1995, when he was succeeded by Peter Schneider. Rams is known for thinking about the designer as a 'silent servant' who gives identities to products but does not impose his own personality upon them. From a background in carpentry and architecture he worked for the architect Otto Apel from 1953 to 1955. Rams's fastidious attention to visual harmony and balance and to the user-related details of his products – such as instrument panels and control knobs – make him one of the twentieth century's most important product designers.

In the early 1960s, the development of transistor technologies radically altered the design of audio products. Previously, large, hot tubes were required to reproduce high-quality sound, whereas now small transistors delivered almost equally true quality. Taking advantage of this, Rams ordered buttons and dials in a logical order and reduced their arrangement to a minimum. The RT-20 tischsuper radio (1961) **right below** uses scale, spacing and a simple grid system to establish functional and visual hierarchy that encourages intuitive use. Like the T1000 world receiver (1963) **right above** it illustrates Rams's belief that design 'can make the product talk. At its best, it is self-explanatory and saves you the long, tedious perusal of the operating manual.'

As a company, Braun was renowned for embracing and encouraging *gute Form* (good design) and produced a company magazine **opposite** that 'spread the word' to all its employees. The covers and content were predominantly about Braun products, such as the Audio 300 **top left**, but from time to time they included other notable examples of good design, including Ettorre Sottsass's Valentine typewriter for Olivetti (1969) **top middle**.

Dieter Rams and the 'Braun style' have influenced a generation of younger designers, among them Jonathan Ive at Apple and the English designer, Jasper Morrison, whom Rams particularly admires. Morrison's Coffee Maker (2004) **above** for Rowenta shares with Rams a rational – almost minimalist – simplicity. There is nothing superfluous to functionality in its form.

One of the most iconic and best-selling of Dieter Rams's designs for Braun is the ET44 calculator (1978) **above middle**. Once again, a rational grid system for the buttons and careful use of colour encourages an intuitive response. This is precisely the ethos that has made Nokia the world's most successful mobile phone manufacturer. The original 6110 (1998) **above right** was a breakthrough at the time in terms of its size, weight and battery life, but equally for the way in which it pioneered a navigation system that remains central to Nokia phones.

DIETER RAMS: 10 COMMANDMENTS

- *GOOD DESIGN IS INNOVATIVE*
- *GOOD DESIGN MAKES A PRODUCT USEFUL*
- *GOOD DESIGN IS AESTHETIC*
- *GOOD DESIGN HELPS US TO UNDERSTAND A PRODUCT*
- *GOOD DESIGN IS UNOBTRUSIVE*
- *GOOD DESIGN IS HONEST*
- *GOOD DESIGN IS DURABLE*
- *GOOD DESIGN IS CONSEQUENT TO THE LAST DETAIL*
- *GOOD DESIGN IS CONCERNED WITH THE ENVIRONMENT*
- *GOOD DESIGN IS AS LITTLE DESIGN AS POSSIBLE*

THINGS WHICH ARE DIFFERENT IN ORDER SIMPLY TO BE DIFFERENT ARE SELDOM BETTER, BUT THAT WHICH IS MADE TO BE BETTER IS ALMOST ALWAYS DIFFERENT. – DIETER RAMS

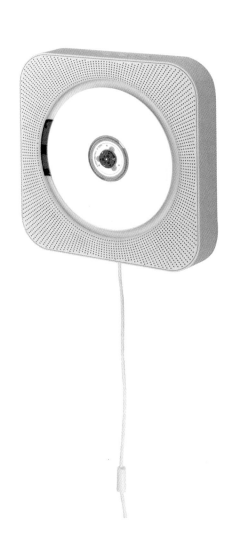

When asked to describe his design style in an interview in 2000, Rams observed, 'In Japanese they say *wabi sabi*: together these two concepts mean "tranquility", "simplicity", "balance" but also "liveliness" and this is a special point of reference for me.'

The Japanese firm Muji has produced a number of highly minimal products which are little more than boxes and which have no additional styling added to them. The cases housing their self-assembly portable speakers **above right** are literally cardboard boxes. Their simplicity and eco-friendliness enhance their primary functionality rather then disguising it. Nato Fukasama's little wall mounted CD player **above left** is one of the most highly lauded products of recent decades. It gets as near as it can to pure functionality without anything getting in the way.

Indeed, for Issigonis, as for Giacosa, the arrangement of the car's interior functional components determined its outward appearance. Issigonis had begun working on the Morris Minor during the war. Its monocoque structure – the use, that is, of its outer shell as its structural support rather than an internal frame – represented a radical departure from the norm and set a new direction for the European car industry. The Minor enabled a family of four to travel in reasonable comfort in a car that was both space- and fuel-efficient. Its curved form was a watered-down interpretation of American streamlining. It went through several face-lifts in the 1950s, its split window disappearing in 1956 and, as larger engines were introduced, its performance was improved.

The Morris Minor was a British automotive icon of the 1950s but Issigonis's Mini became an even more powerful one in the 1960s. He began working on it for the British Motor Corporation (formed by the merger of Morris with Austin) in 1956. The stimulus to create the car came from the fuel shortages produced by the Suez crisis and the competition from bubble cars (tiny, often three-wheeled, usually German-produced cars). His challenge was to create a very small car for four people, plus luggage, that used as little fuel as possible. His design solution was to place the engine in a transverse position, and put the wheels at the extreme four corners, to create the maximum amount of interior space in the minimum body shell. Like the Morris Minor the exterior was a direct result of these decisions and Issigonis produced a timeless design without additional ornamentation or styling. The streamlined curves of the Minor had disappeared, giving way to what was little more than a box on wheels. It quickly became both incredibly popular and the car of choice for pop stars, fashion models and designers and was celebrated as one of the cult objects of 'Swinging London'.

The role of design in other forms of transport in Europe went from strength to strength in the 1960s, culminating in the Concorde aeroplane, an Anglo-French design collaboration, which became one of the lasting icons of the era. The first commercial flight, in 1969, of that supersonic aircraft was the result of nearly twenty years of development that had pushed technological knowledge in the areas of aerodynamics, materials and structures to such a level that completely new solutions were reached. Concorde's strikingly elegant and futuristic nose and wing forms were the result, like those of the Spitfire before it, of decisions based on function- and performance-based criteria. The materials used for this design included titanium, stainless steel and, of course, a variety of plastics.

New inventions
Whereas many consumers living in the industrialised world in the 1950s had been swayed by artefacts that had ornament added to them – such as decorative plastic products and extravagantly styled American automobiles – by the late 1960s a number of objects that were more closely tied to the principles of 'good design' – from chic Italian furniture to the Mini to the engineered Concorde – had succeeded in capturing the popular imagination. The utopian vision of a future world represented by those new, modernist designed objects can be seen as part of the same optimism that put a man on the moon and universally celebrated that momentous achievement. In spite of many young people's attempts to create a more popular, flexible aesthetic, the majority of the population was entranced with modernism's post-war impact and designers' skilled exploitation of the

The Ford Cortina **above**, launched in Britain in 1962, was, as its Italian name wished to suggest, a car with advanced body styling that introduced a new level of visual sophistication on to British roads. A range of different plastics were used for its dashboard, steering wheel, seats and trim **left**, marking it out as one of the first cars to use that material so extensively.

technologies and materials of the post-war world. One of the most important technological breakthroughs of those years was the integrated circuit board, a precursor of the micro-chip that was invented by Jack Kilby in 1958. It made possible, among other things, a new level of product miniaturisation which Japanese manufacturers and designers, in particular, were quick to exploit. Japanese goods, such as Sony's little solid state portable television set of the early 1960s, appealed to consumers through their technological virtuosity. Soon afterwards Japanese designers also began to understand the western concept of 'good design' that they saw being explored in Germany and Italy (and which had, ironically, been strongly influenced by Japanese aesthetics) and the goods they developed from that point were more visually sophisticated as a result.

In post-war Europe plastic products, cars and air travel were on offer to almost everyone and they formed the backbone of 1960s consumer culture. What people failed to realise, was that the fuel that made them all possible would not be cheap forever – nor would it last for ever. With the Arab-Israeli conflict leading to the oil crisis in the early 1970s, oil was suddenly scarce. The shared dream was shattered as a result and the era that followed was utterly different from the one that had preceded it, characterised as it was by an increased scepticism towards technology, by a new focus on the past instead of the future and, above all, by a challenge to designers to bring technology and culture into a new balance with each other. The enthusiasm for market-led design and the importance of consumer taste were renewed as the era of post-modernism, the 1970s and 1980s, replaced the modernism of the 1960s. By the 1990s, however, there was a sense that the party was nearly over and that if design's influence was to survive it needed to find a new role in addressing the numerous challenges – ecological and economic among them – that the new century would bring.

The E-type Jaguar **above** was without doubt Britain's most stylish car of the 1960s. Designed by Malcolm Sayer and chief engineer William Heynes under the close supervision of Jaguar's chairman Sir William Lyons, and launched at the 1961 Geneva Motor Show, the long low lines of its evocative sculptural form gave it an identity that was linked as strongly to its iconic power as it was to its performance. Enzo Ferrari described it as 'the most beautiful car ever made.'

The Sony Walkman personal cassette player, designed and developed by Kozo Ohsone and Nobutoshi Kihara in 1979, transformed the way in which people listen to music forever. Sony invested in a huge marketing campaign to disseminate their radical new product in which they set out to create a market rather than simply to win one. They emphasised the use of the device rather than the compactness of the product itself and commissioned a number of posters that featured people lost in the music they were listening to. This image **right** subtly combines an enraptured girl plugged into her walkman with a text describing the product's innovative nature contained in a magazine floating on an inflatable cushion.

Barbarella (1968) starring Jane Fonda is a quintessentially '60s movie, a sci-fi sex romp based on a popular French comic strip. Film sets and costumes abound with plastics and other synthetic materials, and universal peace is threatened by the evil scientist, Durand Durand, whose accomplished manipulation of the Excessive Machine **following pages**, a 'sex organ', can drive its victim to death by pleasure.

THE CHAIR: PLASTICS

'People buy a chair and they don't really care who designed it,' claimed Arne Jacobsen, in a wild moment. If ever that were true, it is true of the monobloc plastic chair **above**, the scourge of plastic seating and an unlicensed design that is replicated around the world from suburban patios to Mediterranean holiday homes, from street food vendors to Andean cafés. Lightweight, stackable and very cheap to produce, the monobloc is an everyman chair or a disposable eyesore, depending on your point of view. It illustrates perfectly the tensions in design – and especially the use of plastics – between functional mass manufacture and formal 'truth'.

For a certain generation of Britons, the design merits of Robin Day's heroic Polyprop chair (1963) **above right** – whilst clearly inspired by the Eames Plastic Shell chair – are largely obscured by its associations with school assemblies and office meeting-rooms. The polypropylene seat is lightweight, durable, inexpensive and easy to clean, whilst a single-injection mould can produce 4,000 shells a week. Over 14 million Polyprop chairs have been sold over the last 45 years.

But plastics and their potential continue to excite and inspire designers. Antonio Citterio and Oliver Löw's Dolly chair **right below** and Philippe Starck's Mr Impossible (2008) **opposite** – both designed for Kartell – exploit advances in materials and manufacture. Dolly is made from high-strength, fibreglass-reinforced polypropylene to provide maximum loadbearing strength with minimum weight; Mr Impossible, by contrast, invisibly welds two transparent shells to create a piece of furniture of striking simplicity.

SCANDINAVIAN MODERN

The notion that design enshrines national characteristics – German rationalism, English eccentricity, French *savoir faire* or American aspirationalism – is a controversial one. None the less, a number of Nordic architects and designers from the middle period of the twentieth century are widely recognised as 'belonging' to a loose Scandinavian Modern movement. As early as 1939, a room interior at the New York World's Fair by Josef Frank – born in Vienna but long resident in Sweden – was dubbed 'Swedish Modern', and an exhibition of Scandinavian design that toured the US in 1953–5 consolidated the idea of a shared Scandinavian aesthetic. Its defining characteristics were the use of natural materials, organic forms and a certain simplicity or modesty based around domestic spaces and human needs.

One of the movement's key exponents was Arne Jacobsen (1902–71), whose Ant chair (page 146) is an icon of modernism. In 1936, Jacobsen completed the design of a petrol station for Texaco **opposite** that was intended as a prototype, although others were never built. It still stands on the coastal road between Copenhagen and Bellevue in Denmark, although it has been heavily (but sympathetically) restored. The simple, concrete box of the station itself was clad in Meissen ceramic tiles, but the really radical departure is the oval concrete shell that covers the petrol pumps, supported by a single column. That a simple petrol station was ever thus!

It was in the post-war years, however, that Scandinavian Modern gained greatest exposure, even if its merits were temporarily eclipsed by the international success of Italian manufacturers. Per Lutkin's Canada table glasses from the 1950s **above** – for water, wine and schnapps – are elegant in their simplicity and functionality. Norway's most famous designer, Tias Echoff, first rose to international prominence with his Cypress silver cutlery (1953), designed for Georg Jensen and later his Maya stainless steel flatware cutlery (1961) **left**, produced for Norsk Stalpress, in which each piece is reduced to almost elemental simplicity.

BUILDING ART IS A SYNTHESIS OF LIFE IN MATERIALISED FORM. WE SHOULD TRY TO BRING IN UNDER THE SAME HAT NOT A SPLINTERED WAY OF THINKING, BUT ALL IN HARMONY TOGETHER. – ALVAR AALTO

WAYFINDING

Designers play a key role in helping people orient themselves and move from A to B, in a number of different contexts and locations. Wayfinding and signage have become important features of modern life and they influence the appearance of the everyday environment. One important role of design is for it to 'make sense' of an object or environment, to apply the principles of rational order. Unchecked by such principles, signage becomes self-defeating, as in this photograph of Broadway at 45th Street in New York **left** by Andreas Feininger (1954). The multiple signs and theatre placards compete against one another in an ad hoc , uncontrolled manner and create a dynamic, but overly busy and visually over-stimulating environment.

In contrast to the overwhelming sign systems on the streets and avenues of New York, designers have created many directional systems that are hugely helpful to travellers. The British designers Jock Kinneir and Margaret Calvert created a highly ordered and visually clear signage system for Britain's roads which was much admired and became internationally influential. Using carefully coordinated colours, shapes, symbols and lettering – in a clear typeface, Transport, that they designed themselves – they produced wayfinding signs for Britain's new motorways **below left**, in the late 1950s and for all roads in the mid 1960s.

In 1931, the League of Nations convention in Geneva adopted a standardised sign showing a white line in a red circle, known as C1, to denote 'no entry'. Today there are many signs that can be understood regardless of language, including pictograms such as those for the 2008 Beijing Olympics **above**, the joint work of the China Central Academy of Fine Arts and the Academy of Arts and Design, Tsinghua University. The pictograms depict 35 different sports and combine the strokes of ancient Chinese seals with a simple, modern graphic language.

The ubiquity of mobile phone ownership means that it is almost impossible to get lost in many places around the world, as 3G technology allows users to interface with programmes such as Google Maps **below right** that identify the address you are looking for and can even provide instructions on how to get there from your current location.

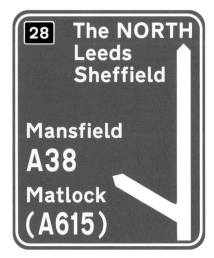

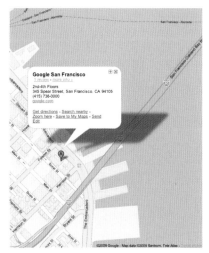

YOUTH CULTURE

ROCK AND ROLL DOESN'T NECESSARILY MEAN A BAND. IT DOESN'T MEAN A SINGER, AND IT DOESN'T MEAN A LYRIC, REALLY. IT'S THAT QUESTION OF TRYING TO BE IMMORTAL. – MALCOLM MCLAREN

Design both creates and responds to changing social cultures. In the postwar years, improved standards of living and education enabled greater social mobility and gave rise to the teenager as a consumer group that used design to create points of difference as well as, within a particular group, to identify shared values.

The American sociologist Talcott Parsons coined the term 'youth culture' in 1942, which he identified as a 'set of patterns and behaviour phenomena' that were unique to the new 'teenage' market, and in January 1945 the *New York Times* Magazine published a 'Teen-Age Bill of Rights' with 10 'Teen Commandments', including 'the right to make mistakes', and 'the right to have fun'. By the 1950s, various sub-cultures used design and dress to articulate membership: in Britain, Teddy Boys – originally called the Edwardians – adopted slicked-back hair and tailored suits, although their uniform was as closely associated with borderline crime as with affiliation to a particular type of music, in spite of some of the characteristics they shared with Elvis Presley and early 'rock & roll' in America.

As more and more niche teenage markets evolved, so the links to emerging musical genres grew. By 1965, Kathy McGowan **below right** was firmly established as 'Queen of the Mods', whose male followers would customise clothes with symbols such as the Union Jack flag and the Royal Air Force roundel; they adopted winklepicker shoes and military parker coats. By the mid- to late-sixties, the Mod scene had largely been overtaken by psychedelic rock and hippy subcultures that prevailed in both Europe and America, although – Hendrix apart – these were largely white phenomena. The civil rights and black power movements of the 1960s and '70s in the US contributed to the emergence of the Afro hairstyle into mainstream culture as an affirmation that 'black is beautiful' and a rejection of Eurocentric notions of beauty. Pop stars such as Stevie Wonder and the young Michael Jackson **below left** embraced the Afro as part of their look.

The do-it-yourself approach to fashion that was championed by punk is perhaps the most enduring – and significant – of the street styles of the last 30 years. Its most successful and controversial exponents, the Sex Pistols, ripped up the rules of dressing and etiquette. Lead singer Johnny Rotten – seen here at the Baton

Rouge Kingfisher Club in 1978 **left** – appropriated safety pins, school uniform and other everyday items to subvert the norm, although many of the most controversial punk clothes were designed and sold by Vivienne Westwood and Malcolm McLaren in their boutique, SEX, on the King's Road in London.

TOMORROW, AND TOMORROW, AND TOMORROW

DESIGN AFTER MODERNISM

1969 saw a man walk on the moon. At the time it seemed to be the ultimate achievement of humankind's relationship with advanced technology. But from the 1970s onwards, the failure of design to deliver the utopian technological vision it had promised us all – robot housekeepers, jetpacks and annual holidays to outer space – put an end to the idealism that had accompanied its journey through the earlier twentieth century. Also many people began to fear that material abundance had brought neither happiness nor fulfilment in its wake, and that the future posed as many threats as it offered promises.

The end of cheap petrol and the economic recession of the 1970s and early 1980s played important parts in this sudden volte-face. Many young people sought alternative, less materialistic lifestyles, sometimes involving a renewed interest in the wartime practice of growing one's own vegetables, making one's own clothes, and doing-it-yourself, helped by publications such as the *Whole Earth Catalog*. People became fascinated, as they had been in the nineteenth century, with the styles of the past. As the obsession with the future dimmed, designers looked back, too.

A temporary global economic boom, within a decade, brought consumerism back to the fore, and designers leapt to service its needs. But by the first decade of the twenty-first century many of the 1970s anxieties had resurfaced and designers had to re-address the challenges that they had temporarily shelved. Ever opportunistic, but at the same time keen to save the world, many designers found themselves seriously questioning their role and motives.

Design went on a circuitous journey in the last four decades, shifting its position as the economy moved from recession to boom and back to recession. Designers returned to the concept of taste and put it back in the home. Rejection of modernism – post-modernism – had a huge impact on design in the 1970s and 1980s, especially in the US and Italy, while the advent of designer-culture found some designers aspiring to the fame and status of fine artists or rock stars. From the 1980s onwards people became increasingly image conscious; this was partly owing to their increasing dependence on finding out about objects primarily through a relationship with flat television and computer screens, rather than experiencing them in three dimensions, but it was also partly because of the general dominance of visual media. Design reflected this, strengthening its hold over lifestyle and finding new spheres in which to apply identity-formation or branding.

By the first decade of the twenty-first century technology had wrought changes in the impact of design, less, perhaps, in terms of the visions offered by industrial designers earlier in the century, but more in terms of an information and communications systems revolution that inevitably drew design into its midst. Most recently, designers have aligned themselves with the problems of over-consumption and renewed their interest in design's social, cultural and ethical roles.

Sky Transport for London (2007) **previous pages** by Professor C.J. Lim, from University College London's Bartlett School of Architecture is a playful vision of a 'sky river' formed by raising London Underground's Circle Line 80 metres/260 feet above ground, along which passengers might travel in environmentally friendly narrow boats – and which could host dragon-boat races. It is Lim's homage to the work of the cartoonist Heath Robinson who was renowned for his spatial inventiveness and designs of fantastic machines.

Dramatic night-time images **opposite** of landmark urban buildings and installations that have become iconic symbols of their cities: fireworks exploding over the National Stadium during the opening ceremony of the Beijing Games in August 2008 **top left**; Philippe Stark immediately made his architectural mark with one of his first buildings, the 'Golden Flame' headquarters of Asahi Breweries, Shiga Prefecture in Tokyo **top right**; architect Tom Wright was asked to make the Burj-al-Arab Hotel (1994) a symbolic statement for Dubai, and designed its dramatic form to resemble the sail of an Arab dhow, using the latest engineering and construction methods **below left**; and a number of New York designers collaborated to make the Tribute in Light (2002), a dramatic memorial to the World Trade Center Twin Towers destroyed by terrorists, in which 88 searchlights create two vertical columns shooting up from the Manhattan skyline **below right**

Less is more

The last two decades of the twentieth century saw a renewed interest in the home as the destiny for consumer goods, as the place where identities were formed and tastes expressed, but also, increasingly, as a financial asset. As a result the terms 'home' and 'property' became interchangeable. Home owners increasingly involved themselves in home improvements as a form of investment. In this they were encouraged by advertising, and helped by the further expansion of mass furniture and furnishings retail outlets, soon joined by the ease of online purchasing.

Expressing one's taste also remained important, however, and design-consciousness in the home became *the* affirmation of the possession of good taste. People sought to learn the differences between good and bad design, finding the necessary information in magazines and TV programmes. Choices of domestic design were on offer in the market place – in modern forms in shops such as Habitat and IKEA – and in retro forms through architectural salvage outlets and flea markets, which required more discrimination on the part of consumers. People became aware of their own roles as designers as they expressed their tastes in their own homes by making design choices.

The word 'design' became increasingly interchangeable with 'taste', and the link between design and social class became more evident. In 1979 the French sociologist Pierre Bourdieu produced his hugely influential *Distinction: A Social Critique of the Judgment of Taste.* Translated into English in the 1980s, it was widely read, not just by academics but by anyone who hoped to discover in its pages what made late-twentieth-century society tick. For Bourdieu taste was no longer the absolute concept promoted by the nineteenth-century British design reformers. Taste was now relative; it revealed the level of education underpinning consumer choices, and, therefore, distinguished one social class from another. Middle-class 'distinction' was now expressed, according to Bourdieu, through a 'less is more' approach while, for the less well educated, it involved an accumulation of material goods. Bourdieu's theory became a lived reality as the fashion for Japanese-inspired minimal interiors spread in the last decades of the twentieth century. The idea that 'good taste' was synonymous with living with as few possessions as possible was heavily influenced by the ultra-simplicity of the domestic spaces created by architects such as John Pawson and Claudio Silvestrin among others.

In the first half of the twentieth century, minimalist architects and designers, such as Gerrit Rietveld and Wells Coates, had believed in the power of design to change behaviour on a permanent basis. However, by the 1980s the dominance of market-led design meant that living in a minimal interior was a lifestyle choice, rather than a serious decision about how life should be lived; it was a choice that was as much aspirational as real, and it could be replaced by another, quite different lifestyle, through a simple decision to redecorate.

Tastemakers

Colour-free and bric-a-brac-free interior spaces filled the pages of fashionable home magazines – from *The World of Interiors* and *Homes & Gardens* to *Wallpaper** in Britain, from *La Maison* to *Elle Décoration* in France, and from *Metropolitan Home* to *Better Homes and Gardens* in the US – and were widely emulated. This could be seen as the logical final destination of pre-war modernism; but it meant that the once highly idealistic design

The 1980s and 1990s saw a number of star designers, style gurus and tastemakers promoting their vision of interior design in new and influential ways. This detail of an accessories station **left** in the B&B Italia store, in London's Brompton Road, displays some of the company's products as if they are almost talismans of style. Designed by John Pawson Architects, celebrated for their minimalist aesthetic, it is set in an interior styled by the Italian designer, Antonio Citterio. A contemporary living-room **right above** illustrated in the publication *Martha Stewart Living* shows the epitome of a tasteful domestic interior as promoted by the American life-style guru. The British 'design' guru and founder of Habitat, Terence Conran, poses for a photograph (1981) in his country home in Newbury, England, to market a look that he successfully brought to aspiring, middle-class consumers.

movement had been stripped of its political mission and transformed into just another one of the many fashionable stylistic options in the marketplace. There was no escaping materialism in this media-driven, post-modern world, where concepts of design and lifestyle were now so inextricably linked.

The link between design and lifestyle was driven by the media and by a number of larger-than-life media figures. One of the most prominent was Martha Stewart in the US, who, in the spirit of the late-nineteenth- and early-twentieth-century domestic advice books, advocated a set of rules relating not only to home decoration but also to gardening, entertaining and self-presentation. In Britain Terence Conran, the founder of the Habitat stores in the 1960s, became an influential 'guru' where ideas about domestic taste were concerned, while, in the same country, figures such as Jocasta Innes and Tricia Guild, and, in France, Andrée Putman, dominated the world of interior decoration, publishing sumptuous 'how-to' books on the subject.

More is not less

Design became increasingly interchangeable with taste and lifestyle in the 1970s and 1980s, and the boundary between design as a professional or as an amateur practice became increasingly blurred. Recognising this, many designers and architects set out to challenge the assumptions that had determined design's progress through the twentieth century. As a result design modernism was replaced by a new movement that avoided judgements about good and bad design, and which acknowledged the importance played by consumption, market values and popular taste.

Back in 1966 the American architect Robert Venturi had set the tone in his publication, *Complexity and Contradiction in Architecture*. This influential text had set out the basic philosophy of what, in the 1970s and 1980s, would come to be called the post-modern movement in architecture and design. 'I prefer', explained Venturi, 'both-and to either-or, black and white, and sometimes gray, to black or white.' He advocated an end to the distinction between high and popular culture and a need for architecture and design to embrace popular values. His words suggested a definition of design that focused on consumption rather than arising from production, which favoured 'form follows expression' over the modernist 'form follows function'. Definitions of good design could now

The first catalogue for the Habitat store was designed by Terence Conran and Stafford Cliff in 1971 and was picked in the early 1990s by *The Sunday Telegraph* newspaper as one of the 'Ten Books that Changed Your Life'. Certainly, the catalogues act as fascinating record of changing styles of life and interior design over the last 40 years. The catalogue for 1999-2000 **above**, designed by SMITH in London, created quite a stir on its release: gone were studio set-ups or photographs of 'perfect' people in 'perfect' homes, to be replaced by photographs of 'real' people living 'ordinary' lives **opposite left**; none the less, in its 'show-and-tell' approach to product listings **opposite right** the catalogue reverts to Conran's original principles.

be inclusive, not exclusive, embracing many styles. In direct opposition to the guiding tenet of modernism Venturi declared 'More is not less'.

Venturi's approach (echoing the thoughts of Elsie de Wolfe nearly half a century earlier) required designed objects to be expressive as well as functional, and opened the floodgates for a new approach to design that delighted in surface pattern, decoration and references to the past. Above all it finally made sense of the challenges that were now confronting designers working with technologically complex objects, such as vacuum cleaners. It had become extremely difficult to apply the modernist principles of 'form follows function' and 'truth to materials' to those multifarious, modern artefacts. Now they were free to use design to make objects visually appealing or to indicate how they could be used rather than having to visually reflect their internal components or their means of production.

Post-modernism made an enormous impact in the US where it enabled a group of progressive architects to discover a new language with which to express themselves. Venturi turned his own words into practice through his collaboration with Knoll International. The result was a set of plastic-laminated, bent plywood furniture pieces available in nine different styles (page 54), from so-called 'Queen Anne' to 'Art Nouveau'. The co-existence of these varied designs, which were manufactured by a single production process albeit with superficial variations, echoed the 'customised mass production' that had been pioneered by General Motors back in the 1920s, and which had put an end to the 'pure' mass production method developed earlier by Henry Ford.

Other examples of 1980s American post-modern design include work by Richard Meier and by the former arch-modernist Philip Johnson. Johnson's New York 'Chippendale' building for AT&T, which featured a pediment inspired by Chippendale bookcases, represented a dramatic change of direction from his earlier modernist designs which had included the ultra-minimalist, Miesian, Glass House he built for himself in New Canaan, Connecticut.

Post-modernism also manifested itself in Italy, its roots going back to the anti-design movement of the 1960s. In his work for the radical design groups Studio Alchimia and Memphis, in the late 1970s and 1980s, the Italian architect-designer, Ettore Sottsass, continued to follow the same path of experimentation that he had set in motion with his 1960s series of prototype wardrobes for Poltronova. Studio Alchimia was an experimental, gallery-based project that used designed objects to focus on the way popular culture used the imagery of high culture. The project brought together innovative and radical work by Sottsass, Alessandro Mendini and others. Mendini's designs were made with a serious purpose. His Kandinsky and Poltrona di Proust chairs (page 234) were quasi-art objects. Both were a re-consideration and a re-working of classic forms, created with a considered and critical intent: this was to express Mendini's views about the impossibility of mass culture not to devalue the power of designed objects. (Although they were articulated a century later, Mendini's views had much in common with those of William Morris.)

The pupose of Ettore Sottsass's work for Studio Alchimia, though still polemical, contrasted with Mendini's, however, and was much more celebratory. His pieces, such as The Structures Tremble table with its 'Pop' colours and its wave-like legs, used innovative furniture forms to demonstrate his view that the imagery of popular culture enriched design.

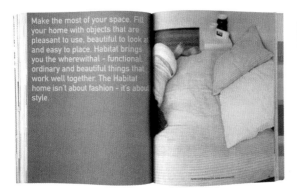
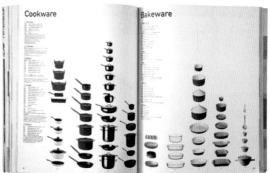

MEMPHIS

Memphis – orignally named The New Design, but rechristened Memphis after the Bob Dylan lyric 'Stuck Inside of Mobile with the Memphis Blues Again' – showed the rest of the world what happened when you put the conventional guidelines about 'good design' to one side. Memphis developed a range of furniture pieces and decorative objects that embraced an emphasis on surface rather than form and which followed the dictum of 'form follows meaning' – what the designer wants to express – rather than 'form follows function'. Led by the designer Ettore Sottsass who had recruited a group of younger designers and international colleagues to work on the radical experiment alongside him, the first exhibition of their work took place in Milan in 1981.

The original exhibition was hugely influential and Memphis items soon filled the pages of the design press across the globe. Its bright colours and surface patterns were widely emulated and were quickly as at home on carrier bags as on chairs. Sottsass's own Ashoka table lamp **right top** is a typically playful design that metaphorically suggests the flow of an electric current. His Carlton bookshelf/room divider **opposite** is one of the most lasting icons of Memphis, as much a playful but powerful, anthropomorphic statement as a utilitarian set of shelves. Michele de Lucchi's Flamingo table (1984) **right middle** revels in similar duality.

Memphis objects were only manufactured as prototypes or made to order and quickly became highly collectable as a result. Key Memphis designers included the Italians de Lucchi, Marco Zanini and Matteo Thun as well as the English designer, George Sowden and the French painter and pattern maker, Nathalie du Pasquier. Zanini's eclectic designs range from the Colorado teapot (1983) **above**, an item so fancifully designed as to be hardly recognisable as a teapot, to the equally visually striking, elegant and functional Dublin sofa (1981) **right**.

SOTTSASS SAID, 'OKAY, LET'S CALL IT MEMPHIS,' AND EVERYONE THOUGHT IT WAS A GREAT NAME: BLUES, TENNESSEE, ROCK'N'ROLL, AMERICAN SUBURBS, AND THEN EGYPT, THE PHAROAHS' CAPITAL, THE HOLY CITY OF THE GOD PTAH. – BARBARA RADICE

I AM A DESIGNER AND I WANT TO DESIGN THINGS. WHAT ELSE WOULD I DO? GO FISHING? – ETTORE SOTTSASS

Following on from the experiments of Memphis, design in the post-modern era used forms that were as unlimited as the designer's imagination; function now dictated nothing. Frank Gehry's Hotel Marqués de Rascal in Elciego, Spain, (opened in 2006) **above** mirrors his even more ambitious Guggenheim Museum in Bilbao. Both demonstrate his deconstructivist approach – the radical, almost gravity-defying use of form – and bear witness to his highly expressive use of metal.

Daniel Weil's Radio in a Bag (1981) **above right** makes the internal workings of this technological object visible thereby rejecting the idea of a simple body-shell concealing its complexity. The cuckoo clock **above far right** by Robert Venturi and his firm for Alessi (although no longer in production), reveals post-modernism's fascination with kitsch and its desire to move away from both good design and good taste.

Following his Plaza dressing table for Memphis – an item of furniture designed to look like architecture – Michael Graves designed this Tea and Coffee Piazza set for Alessi **bottom right** which has the decorative but solid form of neo-classical buildings. It was one of several sets commissioned by Alessi as a promotional project from a range of post-modern architects.

New international style

In 1981 Sottsass, aged over sixty, broke away from the Studio Alchimia experiment to work with a group of young colleagues in the creation of the first Memphis exhibition. Held in Milan, alongside the influential annual Furniture Fair, it presented to the international design press a collection of designed objects that looked shockingly novel and iconoclastic. The global impact of Memphis was immediate. In spite of the fact that they actually owed much to Sottsass's 1960s experiments, and were not, therefore, as 'different' as they may have seemed, in 1981 the Memphis designs represented a radical, new approach.

As well as their unconventional shapes, perhaps the most striking feature of Memphis's objects were the brightly coloured, abstract patterns that were printed on to their laminated surfaces. Much of it was the work of the young French designer, Nathalie du Pasquier, who drew her inspiration from decorative arts from around the world. Her exotic patterns had both a familiar, and a strikingly modern, impact and they succeeded in transforming otherwise simple, utilitarian objects into powerful images.

Whereas Alchimia had been inward-looking, self-reflective and Milan-based, Sottsass's Memphis was outward-looking and international in scope. He dubbed the new movement, with his tongue firmly in cheek, the 'New International Style': this was a dig at 'International Style', the term used in 1932 by the architects Henry-Russell Hitchcock and Philip Johnson to describe modernist architecture. Sottsass was committed to the idea that a retreat from the social engineering programme of modernism in favour of the individualistic approach of post-modernism was a global phenomenon and that it could not be owned by a single country or group of designers. He brought together colleagues from all over the world to participate in his experimental project, from Austria, Britain and Spain to America and Japan.

Japanese design, which had made huge developments in the years after 1950, became influential in the West in the 1980s. Advances in design in that country had been supported by the large corporations – Sony, Sharp, Canon, Hitachi and others – and the Japanese post-war modern architectural movement, led by a group around Kenzo Tange, had achieved international success. By the 1980s, Japan had become a sophisticated consumer society with high expectations of its standard of living and access to lifestyle-affirming goods and services. Japanese manufacturers used design to target niche markets in their efforts to ensure that the whole of Japanese society was engaging in consumption. In the early 1980s, for example, young female consumers were presented with a wide range of feminised goods featuring pastel colours, especially pink, aimed at them. Sharp, for example, introduced the QT50 portable radio-cassette player which – with its curved corners echoing 1930s American streamlined goods, and its plastic body decorated in cream, pale blue, almond green or light pink – was just one of the highly evocative products available to young girls. 1980s Japan had much in common with 1950s American consumer culture, with, that is, the dream kitchens and highly decorated automobiles that had characterised the visual culture of that era.

One country that took the baton on from Memphis in the area of critical, or conceptual, design was The Netherlands. Droog ('dry' in Dutch) Design was a collective, founded in 1993 by the design critic Renny Ramakers and Gijs Bakker – a conceptual jeweller since the 1960s – whose designers included Marcel Wanders, Hella Jongerius, Tejo Remy and Jurgen Bey (pages 226–9).

Philippe Starck's design for the interior of the Lan Club in Beijing (2006) represents his ability to create unique spaces that are both simple and rich at the same time. In this particular environment Starck gave China one of its first post-modern sophisticated interiors that, through its combination of the opulent and the extraordinary, seeks to provide its élite clients with a luxury experience.

They set out to create artefacts that questioned the usual forms and purpose of objects, often in a dryly humorous way. Their designs are deliberately self-referential and witty, and include Remy's Chest of Drawers – a pile of disparate drawers contained by a strap – and Wanders' Knotted Chair – a solid chair that seems to be made of knotted string. Although they started out showing their work in galleries, from 2004 onwards Droog designers also worked to commissions from companies. At the end of the first decade of the twenty-first century Wanders, for example, was also working for a range of international companies, from the long-established Dutch ceramics manufacturer Royal Tichelaar to the Italian furniture firms, B&B Italia and Cappellini. Keen both to shake up design but also to contribute to the everyday environment Droog designers were soon creating provocative and experimental furniture, decorative art objects, consumer products, architecture and interiors that turned traditional ideas about 'good design' on their heads.

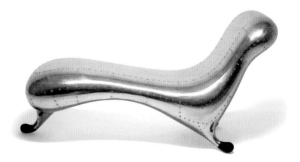

Some people, the English design critic Deyan Sudjic among them, believed that post-modern design was little more than a short-lived, style-led phenomenon – a brief interlude in the otherwise unchallenged domination of modernism through the twentieth century. Indeed, from the second half of the 1980s and throughout the 1990s a number of neo-modernist architectural projects were realised by the likes of Richard Rogers and Renzo Piano. Many designers produced objects in a rigorously geometric, minimal style or in neo-modernist organic forms that recalled the designs of Charles Eames and Eero Saarinen in the years immediately following the Second World War. Neo-modernism had emerged as a counter to post-modernism, re-asserting the modernist principle of form following function and rejecting the playful post-modern affection for the past. However, it was less puritanical and had fewer ideological commitments to determining lifestyles, accepting individual variations on the modern theme. But in an era that embraced difference, diversity and pluralism, modernist styles seemed to co-exist happily enough alongside more eclectic post-modern styles without any serious signs of tension. Design, which had no particular criticism of capitalism, was strongly market-led in these years and absolute judgements – both ethical and aesthetic – were largely suspended. Individuals were therefore free to make their own lifestyle choices.

Old and new

The turn of the century saw a series of stylistic revivals demonstrating the public's growing interest in the recent past. This led to the creation of a number of iconic designs, among them Marc Newson's visually stunning, and hugely costly, aluminium 'Lockheed Lounge' seat of 1986, the riveted metal panels of which recalled the construction techniques of early aircraft. The twentieth century was looking back at itself and reflecting nostalgically upon its own forward-looking technological achievements.

Nowhere was this more visible that in the design of cars. It was demonstrated by Freeman

Marc Newson's Lockheed Lounge seat (1986) is a highly innovative combination of an eighteenth-century chaise longue and a late twentieth-century vision of a metal sitting-object inspired by modern aircraft. Newson made this piece by hand, echoing the methods of traditional aircraft manufacture through his use of multiple rivets to hold the small aluminium sheets together. The result is a flowing, hour-glass form, built over a fibreglass core, that has been described as 'a giant blob of mercury'. Only a few examples of the executed design exist and they command extremely high prices at auction houses.

Thomas and J. Mays's perky new Volkswagen Beetle of the late 1990s; by Bryan Nesbitt's highly nostalgic-looking PT Cruiser, which recalled a whole set of American styling references from 1930s streamlining to post-war hot-rods; by BMW's new 'Mini'; and, most recently, by Fiat's new version of Dante Giacosa's little '500'. In the middle of the twentieth century the car had represented the popular belief in the power of technology, with the help of designers, to construct the future. The 1990s' movement in car retro-styling was able to draw upon the visual languages of the era and rework them at a moment when such a strong faith in the future was absent. These popular retro cars showed that modern design and its consumers were happy to accept a plurality of styles and purposes, sometimes ambiguous, sometimes contradictory.

Superstar design

One of post-modernism's side effects was a popular acceptance of using the name of a designer as a marketing tool and as a guarantor of 'added value'. It reflected the familiar practice of naming fine artists that had been part and parcel of the way in which the market value of art works had been established from the Renaissance onwards, and which was picked up by Josiah Wedgwood in his use of the name of John Flaxman in his product marketing. Within the market economy of the late twentieth century individualism had become a sought-after commodity, and consuming a product with a designer's name attached to it represented a means of asserting individuality (this was, ironically, in spite of the fact that, in doing so, many people were confirming their identities by purchasing exactly the same things and therefore becoming members of the same taste clubs or niche markets).

By the 1980s and 1990s the label 'designer' had been attached to many things especially, and perhaps surprisingly, items of utilitarian dress such as t-shirts and jeans, which were transformed into high-fashion goods, when names such as Giorgio Armani, Gianni Versace, Calvin Klein or Donna Karan were sewn on them.

A number of companies brought in consultant designers to help their attempts to establish upmarket brands. In the 1950s, for example, the Italian furniture manufacturer Cassina had turned to Gio Ponti to help them move from being a supplier of furniture to the Italian navy to working in the open marketplace. Ettore Sottsass had worked in a similar way with the Olivetti company, creating some of that company's leading-edge and most stylish machines. In the following decade Sotsass also worked for Alessi, one of Italy's best-known 'design factories', creating, among other products, an elegant stainless steel oil and vinegar set that bore his name at the point of sale.

The family firm of Alessi is located in a conservative northern Italian valley where it had originally supplied the local population with metal household goods. Alberto Alessi, the grandson of the company's founder, joined the company in 1970, and from the outset he sought to change the company's image by collaborating with architects and designers (as Wedgwood had done two centuries before). Soon after he took over the management of the company in 1979, with his two brothers, Alberto had the idea of commissioning eleven leading international architects to design tea- or coffee-sets for the company. The Tea and Coffee Piazza project included designs by Aldo Rossi, Paolo Portoghesi, Alessandro Mendini, Hans Hollein, Stanley Tigerman, Robert Venturi, Michael Graves and Charles Jencks.

ZAHA HADID

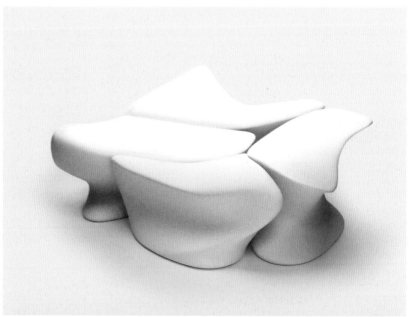

The architect Zaha Hadid (b. 1950) **above** moved into furniture design in the mid 1980s. Her interest was less in creating furniture pieces than in creating unconventional, flowing spaces and her designs mirrored the computer-generated, complex, sculptural forms and fluidity of her architectural compositions.

Her first commission was for the interiors of a house in Cathcart Road, London, and included a coffee table, a detail of which is shown **opposite top right**. The Bitar furniture that developed from that commission, such as the Wave sofa, were large pieces that served to define the spaces they occupied. In 2006 she created her first limited edition of furniture, named Seamless, for London's Established & Sons **right above**. Made of polyester resin the pieces are exercises in the manipulation of space. Three years later Hadid designed a chrome three-way tap (hot, cold and drinking water) for Triflow Concepts **right below**. Demonstrating the same commitment to fluid form, the Cirrus seat (2008) **opposite bottom left** was made of MDF covered with black Formica laminate and was manufactured by Associated Fabrication.

In 2004 Hadid undertook the masterplan design for the first phase of Biopolis **opposite top left**, seven blocks of a biomedical sciences research and development hub on a campus in Singapore. Her complex design for the façade included glass curtain walls, rooftop trellises and sky terraces. Each building was given a unique identity through the use of varied dimensions and contours. In 2003 Hadid designed the Cincinatti Arts Center in Ohio **opposite bottom right**. The entrance is described as an 'urban carpet' which leads visitors up to a suspended mezzanine ramp and into the complex and highly varied exhibition spaces of the building itself.

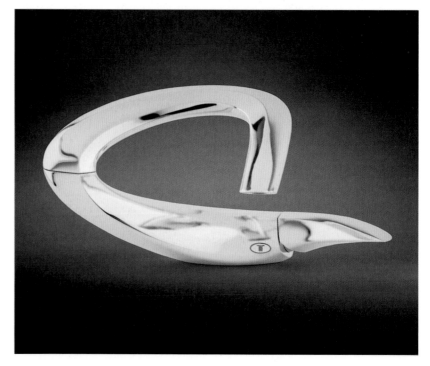

The idea behind the Alessi project was to create works of artistic merit rather than items that would necessarily be functional. The designers' work was intended to be sold directly to museums, thereby short-circuiting the normal process by which museum curators add value to objects by selecting items from the marketplace or the auction room and then including them in their collections.

From this early project Alberto Alessi moved on to commission two world-leading designers – the German (although working in Milan) Richard Sapper, and subsequently the American Michael Graves – each to create a kettle which could be put into production. Two of the late twentieth century's most iconic and dramatically post-modern designs emerged as a result.

Sapper's kettle had a coxcomb-shaped handle and a whistle, shaped like the end of a six-shooter, placed into its spout which emitted the sound of a steam locomotive (a memory from Sapper's childhood) when the water came to the boil. It took Alessi's technicians over a year and a half to perfect the sound. Alberto Alessi has described the kettle as 'polysensorial', explaining that its 'poetical function is the most important.' Graves's design also played on the idea of a 'singing kettle' and featured a bird-shaped whistle (page 105). Neither kettle was designed primarily for everyday use, although nothing prevented that and both were intended to be more functional than the Tea and Coffee Piazza sets. They were, rather, artistic explorations of kettles, along the lines of Gerrit Rietveld's examination of the essence of a chair undertaken six decades earlier. The striking difference between the two, however, was that, while Rietveld's project was a serious, idealistic, modernist exercise in abstract form, Sapper and Graves's kettles exuded a high level of post-pop, post-modern humour.

The Alessi company went from strength to strength from the mid 1980s onwards, collaborating with architects and designers to create, like Josiah Wedgwood had done three centuries earlier, a range of iconic products that sold alongside its more mundane house-wares. One of the company's most celebrated collaborations was with the French 'super-designer' Philippe Starck. They worked together on a number of successful products, including the 'Hot Bertaa' kettle and the controversial 'Juicy Salif' lemon juicer.

In the world of the named designer the self-confident and self-promoting Starck has reigned supreme and taken the identity of the designer as close to that of the fine artist as it can go without actually becoming one. Born in 1949, this son of an aircraft designer undertook his design apprenticeship in the pop-dominated 1960s and set up a firm in 1968 to produce inflatable furniture. A period of time spent working alongside the couturier Pierre Cardin introduced Starck to the relentlessly self-reinventing, self-publicizing and market-focused, designer-led world of upmarket fashion design. He was then highly successful in transferring the insights gained in that world to the hitherto engineering-focused world of industrial design. Like Loewy before him, who had obtained his skills as a self-publicist in the world of advertising, Starck skilfully marketed himself as a brand. By 1982 he had been singled out by President Mitterand to create an interior in the Elysée Palace as part of the President's 'Grands Projets' that brought the role of architecture and design to the attention of the French public.

From the early 1980s onwards Starck's career shot upwards. By the following decade his designs were in demand internationally and he had achieved global recognition. He promoted a

notion of design that demanded that people should look again at the all-too-familiar objects that surround them and redefine their relationships with them. Nowhere was this more apparent than in the designs he created for Alessi. His highly sculptural lemon juicer, for example, which resembles a large spider raised up on extended limbs, sat right on the art/design divide. Like Sottsass's quirky bookcases of the early 1980s, it is also on the functional/non-functional divide, and this has made the design controversial. However, Stark is reported to have said of the Juicy Salif, 'My juicer is not meant to squeeze lemons; it is meant to start conversations.'

Anonymity or celebrity

The strength of designer culture, of the popular idea that designers wield magic wands which can transform lives, reached a peak in the early 1990s. From that point onwards, however, it began to disappear (with just a few exceptions) from view. Many designers chose to withdraw from the spotlight and began to describe themselves as 'humble' and their designs as unassuming. Dieter Rams had proposed a similar role for himself, and for his objects, a few decades earlier. Now designers such as Jasper Morrison, best known for his simple, self-effacing, neo-modernist furniture designs, among them his Ply chair and his

Displaying the same seamless fluid forms as her other designs, Zaha Hadid's Bridge Pavilion for the 2008 Zaragoza Expo **previous pages** confirmed her place as one of the world's leading architects and designers in the early twenty-first century. The innovative design was formed around four pods that acted as structural elements – each intersected and braced each other so that the weight of the bridge was distributed across the four trusses – and as separate spatial enclosures. Its curvilinear external surface was covered by a shark-scale-like permeable membrane that allowed airflow to regulate the microclimate.

Philippe Starck's Juicy Salif lemon squeezer for Alessi (1988) **above left** – perhaps more than any of his designs – displays the fine line between art and design and the aspiration for designed artefacts to do more then merely perform a function. Whatever its efficiency as a kitchen utensil it was often bought as an affordable work of art, as if it were a tamed, domesticated version of one of the huge and powerful Maman sculptures (1999 and onwards), by the American sculptor Louise Bourgeois, seen here in front of Bilbao's Guggenheim Museum **above**.

all-plastic Air chair, adopted a quiet, low-key approach to their roles, and to their restrained and elegant designs. Traditional Japanese ideas about design were evoked. The writer Junichiro Tanizaki's much-discussed essay on aesthetics, *In Praise of Shadows*, which championed the understated and natural, became a cult text for many members of the new generation of designers who were repelled by the idea of 'designer-culture'. In recent years there has also been a return to the idea initially promoted by the Italian 'anti-design' movement of the 1960s, Archizoom and Superstudio among them, that individual designers should work anonymously in collectives. The Spanish duo El Ultimo Grito has successfully worked in this way.

The concept of the named architect or designer did not disappear entirely, however. The architects Norman Foster and Frank Gehry and the designer Ron Arad, among several others, continued to maintain a high level of public visibility in the early twenty-first century and the celebrity of these figures helped to cement the media's interest in design. Following that tradition is the architect Zaha Hadid, who takes the manipulation of space to new levels. Following her studies at London's Architectural Association the Baghdad-born Hadid worked for Rem Koolhaas before setting up her own London-based practice in 1980. She came to public notice through winning a number of international competitions and in 2004 the prestigious Pritzker Architecture prize. Much of her early work was conceptual, but the originality of one of her first realised designs, the Vitra Fire Station in Weil am Rhein in Germany, marked her out as one of the late twentieth-century's most innovative architects. Hadid also moved into design, creating a number of furniture items, among them a range of nine pieces called 'Seamless' in polyester resin,

manufactured by the London-based company Established & Sons. These look like mini architectural exercises, as does her space-age womans' shoe designed for the Brazilian footwear manufacturer, Melissa.

By the twenty-first century, however, other directions in the designer's relationship with society and culture had begun to emerge, among them the increasing importance of multi-disciplinary teams, and the application of what came to be called 'design thinking' to challenges beyond those linked to product manufacturing. Design and designers began to move away from their traditional links with industry and to apply their skills to services and to a wide range of other areas of business or social enterprise. In countries such as China, Taiwan, Korea, Singapore and India, which were late arrivers on the design scene, designers are able to work on a number of levels, both with manufacturing industry and as part of multi-disciplinary, problem-solving teams working on a range of issues ranging from the financial to the health sectors.

New materials, new technologies, new design

In the decades after 1970, people's faith in technology as the engine for achieving a problem-free, perfectly designed world was at an all-time low. However, huge advances were made in electronics and new materials that, in conjunction with design, dramatically changed the way we live our lives on a daily basis. The jury is still out as to whether the expanded opportunities we've been given – especially to access information and to communicate with each other – are, ultimately, a help or a hindrance. The invention of the microchip, and the radical possibilities for miniaturization that flowed from that world-changing development, gave birth to the MP3 player and the lap-top computer, and to our need

Collect all five.

The advertising campaign for Apple's famous iMac computer represented a turning point in the public's acceptance of home computers. For the first time the machine was presented as a decorative domestic accessory. The 1999 advertisement **left** humorously suggests that the different gumdrop colour versions of Jonathan Ive's design are so desirable that computer users will want them all.

Sportswear design and fitness in general were important themes in the 1980s and 1990s, spurred on by new materials. The body of American Tony Benshoof – in action during the training for the 40th Luge World Championships at the Rodelbahn Oberhof in 2008 **right** – looks like an efficient, streamlined machine which has become merged with the luge itself. Benshoof's success, like those of swimmers, cyclists and other speed athletes, is hugely dependent upon the aerodynamic qualities of his sportswear.

to be constantly entertained and/or accessing data; while advances in plastics research facilitated the emergence of complex products.

The story of sportswear, for example is one of continual research and development into new materials, especially in the creation of sports footwear. But in addition to this, manufacturers such as Nike and Adidas have evolved a strong cultural grasp of people's changing lifestyles, and have employed design to erode the boundary between everyday clothing and specialist sportswear, so that today trainers and jogging pants are marketed to and bought by people who have no particular interest in taking any exercise.

Innovation and desire

No single electronics company has brought technology into contact with lifestyle more successfully than the US's Apple Computers. From the beginning its founders, Steve Jobs, Steve Wosniak and Ronald Wayne, set out to make computers user-friendly. Their interest in the design of their products was there from the beginning and was consolidated by Jobs's relationship, in the mid 1980s, with the designer, Hartmut Esslinger, head of Germany's frogdesign. Esslinger made the radical suggestion that Apple should make white computers rather than, as was the industry norm for all electronic goods at that time, black ones, and he used the 'Snow-white' design language to style all Apple products, first creating the light beige 'Apple II' which put the company on the map as a design innovator.

Apple's reputation was taken to a new level with the relationship it subsequently formed with the British designer Jonathan Ive, who moved to the west coast of the US in 1992. Six years later saw the launch of the hugely innovative iMac computer. Its dramatic organic form and range of stunning translucent colours made it look more like a piece of jewellery or candy (Ive himself claims to have been influenced by the colours of gumdrops) than a piece of computer hardware. The first 'Bondi Blue' model was introduced in 1998, but was replaced by a new range of other vibrant colours in the following year, Grape, Tangerine, Lime, Strawberry and Blueberry among them. The iMac was a three-dimensional object for which the back was as carefully considered as its front, a dramatic change from the norm in styling technological hardware. It was the first computer design that addressed its appearance as an object in an environment as well as an item of advanced technology. Ive's rigorous re-design process also ensured that the iMac looked like a portable object; that it was unapologetically made of plastic; that it was quiet in use; and that, above all, it was easy to use.

From the late 1990s onwards Ive went on to create a range of equally radical designs for Apple, from the non-translucent version of the iMac, modelled, in its ability to rotate by 360 degrees, upon a sunflower, to the iconic iPod and the iPhone. His simple, yet highly sophisticated approach has helped make Apple Computers a leader in their field and, most importantly, to prove that high technology can, through design, be given a human face. Above all Ive understands the crucial and complex relationship between people and objects and he sets out to make that interaction straightforward, easy and natural in spite of the mysterious, high technology world we all inhabit.

Although high investment in research and development underpins the success of technological products, good design is crucial. It played an important role, for example, in the British designer-engineer James Dyson's invention, the bagless vacuum cleaner. The

No other sportswear item could compete with the trainer in terms of technological complexity and sophistication of design. Although now worn by ordinary people merely as a comfortable shoe and – in the case of the latest designs – as a fashion statement, their primary purpose was for athletes. The bespoke gold running shoes by Puma for the Jamaican sprinter Usain Bolt became an icon of the 2008 Beijing Olympics.

G-Force machine that Dyson developed, later known as the 'Cyclone', used cyclonic separation to suck up dirt and dust. This was indeed revolutionary for a vacuum cleaner, but its success was as much a result of its novel design – the arresting use of cheerful yellow plastic, and the transparent shell which lets you see the dirt being picked up – as of the technological innovation it built upon. Like Ive, Dyson, a former art student, understands the need to make technology 'friendly' (and, arguably, 'feminine') and he added a range of colours – pink when it was being made in Japan, and, later, a whole spectrum of other bright colours – to make that possible.

New identities, new brands

Design and technology could not have worked together so successfully if their relationship had not been linked with branding. Apple's logo was all-important, as indeed logos are to a host of products, particularly trainer brands such as Nike. Branding depends on more than logos, however. In the years after 1970 the definition of design expanded to include the part it played in identity formation, whether of corporations or of individuals – or even of cities or nations. During the same years people came to be understood not just as consumers but more as members of particular 'taste cultures', defined by age, class, gender, ethnicity, or simply by common interests and values. The identities formed by taste cultures are predominantly food, clothing and lifestyle focused and increasingly design plays a role within all three areas. Indeed, in the early twenty-first century, food design, or the arrangements of the components of a meal on a plate, has become one of the ways in which everyone can become designers, guided, as in the creation of their domestic interiors, by television programmes and advice books on the subject.

Design can create identity on a plate or in a metropolis. Several cities re-branded themselves – that is, tried to establish separate, fashionable and exciting identities – in this period. Notable among them was Barcelona, where the local government and industry joined hands to create a new, stylish urban environment. Following the collapse of the Fascist regime in the 1970s Spain initiated a programme of modernization. Catalonia sought to differentiate itself from the rest of Spain, however, and to build on its early twentieth-century reputation as a centre for modern design, based on the work of Antoni Gaudi and his contemporaries, and its strong industrial infrastructure. More importantly Barcelona also understood the importance played by consumption and meeting the needs of a new, wealthy middle-class market – in its new self-identity. Designed goods and spaces were fundamental elements of contemporary Barcelona and the city saw the rise of a fresh generation of furniture and product designers who quickly became successful globally, among them Oscar Tusquets and Javier Mariscal, who contributed significantly to that new vision.

Since Barcelona's well-documented re-branding exercise many other cities, including some Eastern European centres, Budapest and Prague among them, have gone down the same path. Much of the wealth of Middle Eastern countries, such as the United Arab Emirates, has also been invested in new material infrastructures; the UAE's Dubai and Abu Dhabi have set out to build some of the world's tallest buildings in their bids to become important modern places. Shanghai has seen a similar transformation. Urban brands co-exist, therefore, with corporate brands and compete for attention in our brand-saturated, contemporary global environment.

MARCEL WANDERS

Marcel Wanders **above** is a designer whose quirky approach and irreverence has brought demand for his work from architects, manufacturers and retailers around the world. Born in the Netherlands in 1962, Wanders graduated from the School of Arts in Arnhem in 1988 and quickly became a prominent member of the Dutch group of Droog designers, for whom he created his Knotted Chair (1996) which gained global attention and became iconic of an approach that valued handcraft, simple materials and the realization of conceptual ideas in material form.

His Sponge vase (1997) **top left** – like Studio Libertiny's Made by Bees vase (page 29) – draws on extraordinary technology to create a porcelain object without using a mould. Wanders developed a technique that allowed him to dip a natural sponge in fluid porcelain which then impregnates the dry sponge. After firing, the sponge 'disappears' to leave a perfect copy in porcelain. A similarly creative approach to form and materials is evident in his Crochet light **middle left**, designed as a personal edition, and Crochet table **bottom left**, designed for his company, Moooi (both 2001).

In 2006, the Italian lighting company Flos re-issued its famous Cocoon lamps, designed in the 1960s by Achille Castiglioni, and invited Wanders to design a new lamp, which he called the Cocoon Zeppelin **top right**. The little Egg speaker (2005) for HE (Holland Electro) **middle right** is part of a set of hi-fi pieces that add decoration to home entertainment – the antithesis of Dieter Rams' approach at Braun – whilst Wanders' I Hate Camping range for Puma (2007), including luggage **bottom right**, is similarly irreverent. Wanders' designs range from expensive one-offs to the mass market, such as the digital wallpaper he created for Habitat in 2007 **opposite** as part of a series that also includes designs by Matthew Williamson and Barbara Hulanicki.

IT IS OUR RESPONSIBILITY TO BE MAGICIANS, TO BE JESTERS, TO BE ALCHEMISTS, TO CREATE HOPE WHERE THERE IS ONLY ILLUSION, TO CREATE REALITY WHERE THERE ARE ONLY DREAMS. – MARCEL WANDERS

In many ways, Wanders and his Droog colleagues breathed new life into the design world, using shock tactics similar to those of the Surrealist artists in the early twentieth century. These young Dutch designers challenged conventions and constantly blurred the boundaries between art and design.

Sander Mulder's punning Woofer speaker system (2009) **opposite top left** adds desirability – in the form of a useful function – to an otherwise grotesque object, the headless dog. Tord Boontje's Garland **opposite top right**, designed for Habitat in 2002, turns a light into an art object. It is a laser-cut length of metal flowers and leaves which attaches around a light fitting; the petals and leaves catch on to each other and form the shade in a similar but unique way for every installation.

Jurgen Bey and Maarten Baas set out to subvert expectations in their designs. Bey transforms ordinary objects into the extraordinary. His Kokon furniture (1999) **opposite bottom** is a skeleton of existing furniture pieces wrapped in a tight PVC sheath which shrinks to form a smooth elastic skin. The design of his knitted or 'Little Prince' chair (2008) **below right** deliberately uses a material covering that doesn't quite fit. Each piece of Maarten Baas's Sculpt furniture (2007), such as the cupboard **below left**, begins as a quick sketch which Baas reproduces as fine furniture, deliberately keeping the original crooked form, but on a monumental scale.

While, as we have seen, some companies identify themselves by promoting the names of the designers with whom they work, others adopt the Coca-Cola principle of putting the company name first. Traditionally, Japanese corporations and car manufacturers have played down the names of their mostly in-house designers, choosing to present their company names as brands instead. That is changing gradually, and the names of a select few automotive designers, BMW's Christopher Bangle among them, have recently been made visible to the public through the media. However, as ecological issues become increasingly significant, that trend may fade.

Designing the future

In the post-modern era design continues to be defined by characteristics formed back in the nineteenth century. Those are: its links with industry; its relationship with marketing and the marketplace; its pre-eminence in the home and its role in identity formation; its close links to taste and social status; its role as an interface between technology and people; and its important function as an agent of cultural change. Recent years have seen design exploring disparate directions, with the celebrity-designer as part of a new 'designer-culture', and with a role in the expansion of the concept of branding. Longstanding disciplinary barriers have been eroded – fashion designers, Giorgio Armani, Ralph Lauren and Calvin Klein for example, have moved into home-wares and interior design – while the gap between high and mass culture has also disappeared as many fashion designers, such as John Galliano, Jean-Paul Gaultier and Vivienne Westwood, take their inspiration from the street. The long-protected divide between, on the one hand, design as a professional activity and, on the other, an amateur undertaking, has been further challenged by the capacity of computer software programmes to allow everyone to become his/her own graphic designer. Unending debates take place among graphic design professionals who feel that there is still a place for high level skills in this area. Equally some leading graphic designers, such as the Englishman, Neville Brody, have embraced the challenges of computer software.

The computer has radically challenged the world of design in numerous ways. The growth of interaction design, for example, has taken design further into the world of the virtual and the conceptual, and is incrementally eroding design's boundary with fine art. Computer-aided design has transformed the nature of the design process in the areas of architecture and product design. The path established by the Jacquard loom back in the nineteenth century has led to the development of computer-controlled manufacturing, including rapid prototyping.

Another recent change in our understanding of design has been influenced by our growing awareness of the vulnerability of the world's natural resources and of the effects of over-consumption. While this is a challenge, first and foremost, for politicians, designers have become conscious that they can play a part by using sustainable materials, by ensuring that their products can be disassembled as easily as they can be assembled, and, most importantly, by designing products that will last. Sustainability has become a design mantra, a sine qua non of designing, and it will undoubtedly continue to influence design for many years to come. However, while on the one hand there is a growing suspicion of consumption for consumption's sake and, in some quarters, a return to wartime 'making do and mending', on the other it is recognised that it is simply unrealistic to expect populations in developing

Many of the designs of the Turkish-Cypriot-born Briton Hussein Chalayan, such as his skirts that transform into tables, blur the distinction between fashion and conceptual art installations. Here a pair of puffy, helium-filled black balloons float above a model, attached to her via a black gymslip/harness combination, and suggesting a fantasy in which fashion could literally transport the wearer to another world.

Calvin Klein
home

dedicated to home interiors, food and fashion bear witness to people's growing appetites for personalised images, objects and spaces. But design will continue to form and reflect our lives in the future, whether by influencing us as we buy a cushion for a sofa or through the prototyping, by a professional designer, of a new mobile phone with new functions.

Design now has different guidelines. On the one hand, there is the 'anything goes as long as it is expressive' approach to taste: a product of our replacing the production-led rules of modernism with the consumption-determined free-for-all that is post-modernism. On the other, the ecological and financial challenges we all face are establishing a new set of rules or ethical criteria. In addition, on the public and practical level rather than the private, we continue to need designers more than ever before – to create our prosthetic limbs and aortic heart valves; to help us to orient ourselves as we move from place to place; and to interpret for us the advances in complex technologies that are beyond our understanding and to make it easy for us to use them in our daily lives. Design is as central to our lives as it has always been and it will undoubtedly continue to be so. While in one way we can all be designers, in another we are as dependent as ever upon educated and experienced professionals with their highly developed creative and communicating skills. Indeed such are the complex demands on designers today that they need an ever broader knowledge and skills base. We may no longer have a simple formula for 'good design', but the social, political cultural, aesthetic and ethical ideas expressed by William Morris a century and a half ago are still ringing in our ears and will undoubtedly help us develop a definition of design relevant for the challenges of the twenty-first century.

parts of the globe to deny themselves the, as yet not-experienced, pleasures of the acquisition of goods, the excitement of the jostling that comes with social mobility, and the need for everyone to create his/her own self-identity through the application of taste in the marketplace.

Product manufacturing and the process of designing have been dramatically transformed in the new age of information and automation. However, perhaps the greatest impact on design has come from the expansion of the mass media and its influence on the formation of taste. The expanding number of television programmes

American fashion designers, in particular, have used their brands to extend their product ranges from clothing and fragrances to interiors. Typography apart, there is little to link the Calvin Klein Home range **above** with its iconic advertising for scent and underwear, although the muted palette of colours reflects the sober designs of its mainline clothes collections.

At the 2009 Milan Furniture Fair, fashion houses unveiled some show-stopping new homeware, from Armani's 24-carat gold plate Adelchi writing desk to Diesel's Successful Living collection. Perhaps the most playful approach came from Maison Martin Margiela, the fashion house founded by Belgian-born Margiela. Images from the company's old Paris atelier were photo-printed on to wallpaper and rugs **right** to create large-scale *trompe l'oeil* pieces.

THE CHAIR: HOMAGE

The post-modern design movement of the 1970s and 1980s brought with it a chance to revisit modernism and to reinterpret many of its idealistic statements within a more ironic, eclectic climate.

Seen here are two designs by the Dutch designer, Maarten Baas: the Plastic Chair in Wood **middle right** of 2008 and the Smoke-Rietveld Chair **opposite** of 2004; both revisit classic modernist designs. One is the ubiquitous monobloc plastic chair (page 192) which Baas had produced by Chinese woodcarvers using traditional techniques. The other is the heroic Red/Blue chair by Gerrit Rietveld (page 85) of several decades earlier here re-imagined as part of Baas's Smoke furniture, where pieces are burned with a blowtorch and then preserved in a clear epoxy coating.

An earlier revisiting and commentary on a classic modernist icon was the Italian designer Alessandro Mendini's redesign of Marcel Breuer's Wassily chair (1978), its austere lines decorated with playful patterns **bottom right**. In his evocation of Marcel Proust, the Poltrona di Proust (1978) **right top** he appropriated a ready-made replica of an eighteenth-century armchair and covered the fabric and wooden parts with a pattern from a painting by the pointillist-impressionist artist Paul Signac, thus, as he says, 'dissolving the shape into a kind of nebula.' His intention was 'to make a culturally grounded object based on a false one' (the kitsch, mass-produced fake antique chair). Both Mendini chairs were created in 1978 for Studio Alchimia.

SPONTANEITY IS MISSING IN SO MANY RATIONALIZED PRODUCTS THAT GO FROM A SKETCH, TO A COMPUTER RENDERING, TO A PROTOTYPE AND AT THE END, THERE IS NO HEART AND SOUL ANYMORE. – MAARTEN BAAS

A QUESTION OF TASTE

One of the ambitions of post-modernism was to do away with the hierarchical distinctions that had existed within modernism and to let bad taste play as important a role as good taste in the world of design. The new designers of the 1980s and 1990s were quick to grasp the freedom that came with an exploration of the previously outlawed conventions of bad taste and ventured into hitherto taboo areas with great enthusiasm and delight.

Philippe Starck's gnome stool for Kartell – the Attila Stool Table **above right** – (which is no longer in production) was one such example. In 2007 Marcel Wanders also explored the world of tastelessness in his series of five different Airborne Snotty vases which are based on three-dimensional scans of airborne snot, such as Coryza **above**. The forms of Wanders's vases bear an uncanny resemblance to Stephen Johnson's sculpture in resin **opposite** from the Now Isn't That Lovely series in which kitsch objects of animals and birds are joined together.

In 2001 the British store Habitat wittily combined a lavatory roll holder with a newspaper rack and called it One Line **right**.

GRAPHIC LANGUAGES

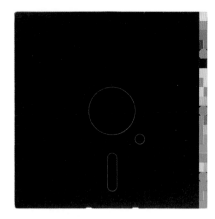

Typography underwent changes over the last four decades like all other aspects of design. The American graphic designer Milton Glaser's I Love New York logo **top right** of 1977, built on his pop graphic work of the previous decade. It has been consistently used since then to promote tourism in New York. Nearly two decades later Glaser has added political engagement to his involvement with popular culture. His striking Darfur poster **middle far right** of 2006, was created for the International Rescue Committee. His OhBAMA Reason 3 forms part of the 30 Reasons email and internet campaign (2008) to encourage people to vote for Barack Obama. Thirty graphic designers each created a poster giving one reason why people should vote for him.

Alan Fletcher's 1993 strikingly simple poster for a design congress **bottom near right** used a found label and a hand-written slogan, while in his poster for Gitanes **bottom far right** he computer-manipulated the image of Max Ponty's iconic gypsy to make her own shadow.

The Austrian-born Stefan Sagmeister's poster for the American Institute of Graphic Artists's Fresh Dialogue talks in New York of 1966 **opposite top** uses an obvious concept of tongues overlaying hand-written text, though the use of phallic-looking cow's tongues makes the image fresh.

The British graphic designer Neville Brody's designs for The Face **opposite bottom left,** showing the distinctive dropped triangular A in the masthead, were hugely influential in magazine design in the 1980s. Described as looking like 'MySpace in print', Super Super is one of the new generation of style magazines.

Peter Saville's design for New Order's 12-inch single Blue Monday **above** is notable, among other striking features, for having no typography at all. The colour coding at the edge 'spells' the name of the band and track.

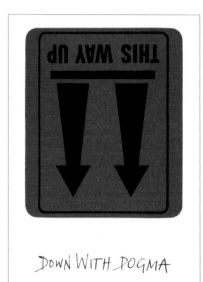

a homage to Max Ponty

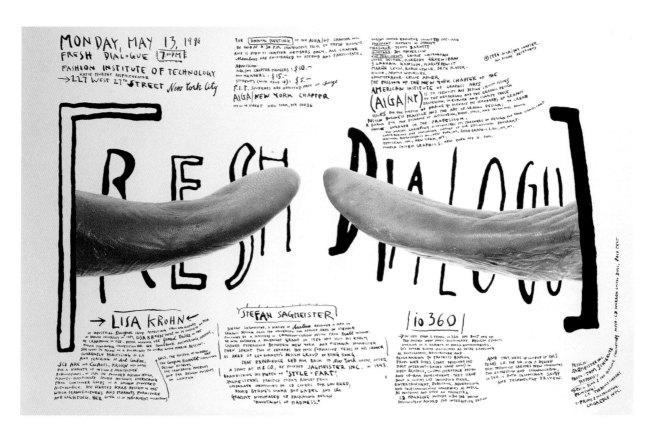

BRANDED CITIES

From the 1990s onwards a number of cities across the globe began to understand how they could use architecture and design to create new, modern identities for themselves. Often this environmental re-branding coincided, as it did in Barcelona and Beijing, with a major tourist event such as the Olympic Games.

The Petronas Towers in Kuala Lumpur **above** were constructed as an expression of Malaysia's culture and history and as a symbol of its rapid economic growth. Pelli Clarke Pelli Architects integrated Malaysian craft into their design and the idea of the step-backs that form part of the structure of the towers is borrowed from traditional Malaysian architecture.

Mumbai is a city that also boasts huge towers as markers of economic success **right** as the character Salim points out in Danny Boyle's hugely successful film *Slumdog Millionaire*. The film also shows the other side of Mumbai which is in marked contrast to the showy optimism depicted here.

Shanghai's Pudong skyline, with the Oriental Pearl Television Tower, situated near the Huangpu River, as a prominent feature, is a strikingly futuristic cityscape **top right** on land that only 30 years ago was largely undeveloped. The 2007 BMW World distribution centre in Munich **opposite above**, designed by architect Wolfgang Prix, is both a dramatic architectural statement and an extension of the car company's successful brand.

The city of Las Vegas is represented by its highly symbolic architecture that has reconstructed the iconic architecture of the Old World – from the Pyramids and Ancient Rome, to Venice and the Eiffel Tower **opposite below** – in a desert in the New World.

WE USED TO LIVE RIGHT THERE, MAN. NOW IT'S ALL BUSINESS. INDIA IS AT THE CENTRE OF THE WORLD NOW, BHAI. – SALIM, SLUMDOG MILLIONAIRE (2008)

GREEN AGENDAS

The turn of the twentieth to the twenty-first century saw an increasing emphasis upon the environment and a growing anxiety relating to the rapid depletion of the world's natural resources. Designers became increasingly conscious of these issues along with everyone else and sought ways of addressing them through their work. From fashion to car design and architecture, strategies were developed by designers to help in the slowing down of the depletion of resources and in finding alternative ways of making and building.

The silk dress designed by Donna Karan **above** for the Earth Pledge Future Fashion show in 2008 has been tea-stained to avoid the use of synthetic dyes. Marco Aurelio Galán Henríquez's electric Hyperion concept car of 2008 **right** directly addresses the problem of the greenhouse gases that increasingly fill the atmosphere. The car's lightweight body, made of carbon-fibre-reinforced plastic, minimises the amount of power needed to drive it.

Stuart Haygarth's Tide Chandelier from 2009 **above right** is made from debris washed up on a stretch of the Kent coastline. Only clear and translucent objects are integrated into this design. Although different in size and shape they are beautifully united to form a sphere, representing the moon which causes the tides that wash up the debris.

Singapore's Nanyang Technological University's School of Art, Design & Media's building (2006) **right above** has been carefully integrated into the wooded landscape that

surrounds it. Its turfed roofs which slope down to ground level help to integrate the building visually with its environment, to replace the land that has been removed to create the building, to provide a form of natural insulation that helps keep the building warm in winter and cool in summer and to offer a habitat for insects and other forms of wildlife.

A parking structure in Santa Monica's Civic Center (2005) **right bottom** designed by Moore Ruble Yudell Architects & Planners is not only stylish but also sports a number of green

credentials, among them photovoltaic panels on the roof and on three façades, natural ventilation and illumination and the use of recycled construction materials.

VIRTUAL WORLDS

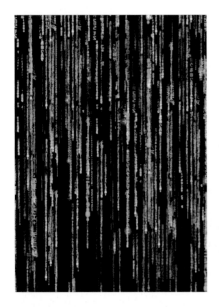

Increasingly we all inhabit not only a visual, material and spatial world but also a virtual one. Indeed it is in this last environment that many of our fantasies and desires are being most fully lived out, through films and videos but also, most importantly, through interactive games. Interaction design is the one of the newest and fastest growing fields of design.

The Wachowski brothers' film *The Matrix* (1999) takes the notion of virtual reality into a nightmare future. Here most humans are plugged into a computer network – the Matrix, which is represented on computer screens by the 'falling rain' green code **above** – and live unknowingly in a virtual world that proves to be far from real.

Google Earth lets its users 'fly anywhere on Earth' by using its virtual globe, map and geographic information program, in which you can view satellite imagery, maps, terrain and buildings in three dimensions. In the image **top right** it is tracking hurricane Gustav across the Gulf of Mexico. Its three-dimensional recreation of Ancient Rome lets you take a virtual tour of the Coliseum **near right**.

Computer games, too, pull their players into a virtual reality. Grand theft Auto IV, set in Liberty City – a virtual New York – **far right** is the most realistic yet of the series, and allows users to compete with multiple players online. In the virtual world of Spore **opposite** players control the evolution of a species from a microscopic organism **above** to a complex organism **below** – and can then develop it further as an intelligent social being, then on to mastery of the planet and beyond into space.

THE HOUSERS [GRAND THEFT AUTO DESIGNERS] ARE CREATING TAPESTRIES OF MODERN TIMES AS DETAILED AS THOSE OF BALZAC OR DICKENS. – MATT SELMAN, TIME 100 (2009)

FURTHER READING

General

Attfield, J. *Wild Things: The Material Culture of Everyday Life* (Oxford and New York: Berg, 2000)

Aynsley, J. *A Century of Graphic Design* (London: Mitchell Beazley, 2001)

Breward, C. *Fashion* (Oxford: Oxford University Press, 2003)

Doordan, D. P. *Twentieth-Century Architecture* (London: Lawrence King, 2001)

Dormer, P. *The Meanings of Modern Design: Towards the Twenty-First Century* (London: Thames and Hudson, 1990)

Forty, A. *Objects of Desire: Design and Society 1750-1980* (London: Thames and Hudson, 1986)

Foster, H. *Design and Crime (and other diatribes)* (London and New York: Verso, 2002)

Heskett, J. *Toothpicks and Logos : Design in Everyday Life* (Oxford: Oxford University Press, 2002)

Julier, G. *The Culture of Design* (London: Sage, 2000)

Loewy, P. *Never Leave Well Enough Alone* (New York: Simon and Schuster, 1951)

Massey, A. *Interior Design of the 20th Century* (London: Thames and Hudson, 1990)

Sparke, P. *As Long as It's Pink: the Sexual Politics of Taste* (London: Pandora, 1995)

Woodham, J. *Twentieth-Century Design* (Oxford: Oxford University Press, 1997

Chapter One

Burckhardt, L. *The Werkbund: Studies in the History and Ideology of the Deutscher Werkbund* (London: Design Council, 1980)

Dolan, B. *Josiah Wedgwood: Entrepreneur to the Enlightenment* (New York: HarperPerennial, 2008)

Greenhalgh, P. (ed) *Art Nouveau 1890-1914* (London: V&A Publications, 2000)

Halen, S. *Christopher Dresser* (London: Phaidon, 1990)

Hounshell, D. *From the American System to Mass Production* (Baltimore: The John Hopkins University press, 1985)

Naylor, G. *The Arts and Crafts Movement: A study of it sources, ideals ands influence on design theory* (London: Studio Vista, 1971)

Chapter Two

Beecher, C. & Stowe, H.B *The American Woman's Home* (New York: J.B. Ford and Co., 1870)

Dreyfuss, H. *Designing for People* (New York: Viking Press, 1955)

Frederick, C. *The New Housekeeping: Efficiency Studies in Home Management* (New York: Garden City, Doubleday Page, 1913)

Naylor, G. *The Bauhaus Re-Assessed: Sources and Design Theory* (London; Herbert Press, 1985)

Sparke, P. *The Modern Interior* (London: Reaktion, 2008)

Teague, W.D. *Design This Day: The Technique of Order in the Machine Age* (London: Studio Publications, 1946)

Troy, N. *The De Stijl Environment* (Cambridge, Mass: The MIT Press, 1983)

Chapter Three

Drexler, A. *Charles Eames: Furniture from the Design Collection* (New York: Museum of Modern Art, 1973)

Goodden. H *Camouflage and Art: Design for deception in World War II* (London: Unicorn Press, 2007)

Handley, S. *Nylon: The story of a fashion revolution* (Baltimore: the John Hopkins University Press, 1999)

Jentz, T. L. *Germany's Tiger tanks: Germany's Tiger tanks DW to Tiger 1 Design, production and Modifications* (Berlin: Schiffer Publishing, 2004)

Mills, J. *Utility Furniture of the Second World War: The 1943 Utility catalogue with an explanation of Britain's Second World War Utility scheme* (London: Sabrestorm Publishing, 2008)

Chapter Four

Alison Clarke *Tupperware: the Promise of Plastics in 1950s America* (Washington and London: Smithsonian Institution Press, 1999),

Jackson, L. *The New Look: Design in the 1950s* (London: Thames and Hudson, 1991)

Jackson, L. *The Sixties: Decade of Design Revolution* (London: Phaidon, 2000)

Katz, S. *Plastics: Design and Materials* (London: Studio Vista, 1978)

Kaufman, M. *The First Century of Plastics* (London: Plastics Institute, 1963)

Sparke, P. *Italian Design* (London: Thames and Hudson, 1988)

Sparke, P. 'Plastics and Pop Culture' in Sparke, P. (ed.)*The Plastics Age: From Modernity to Postmodernity* (London: V&A Publications, 1990), pp. 92-104

Chapter Five

Alessi, A. *The Dream Factory: Alessi since 1921* (Milan: Electa/Alessi, 1999)

Dormer, P. (intro) *Jasper Morrison: Designs, projects and drawings 1981-1989* (London: Architecture and Technology Press, 1990)

Foster, H. *Postmodern Culture* (London: Pluto Press, 1990)

Horn, R. *Memphis: Objects, Furniture and Patterns* (New York: Simon and Schiuster, 1986)

Papanek, V. *The Green Imperative: Ecology and Ethics in Design and Architecture* (London: Thames and Hudson, 1995)

Sparke, P. *Japanese Design* (London: Michael Joseph, 1987)

Sudjic, D. *Ron Arad* (London: Lawrence King, 1999)

Sweet, F. *Philippe Starck: Subverchic Design* (London: Thames and Hudson, 1999)

PICTURE CREDITS

The publisher has made every effort to trace the photographers and copyright holders, and we apologise in advance for any unintentional omission, and would be pleased to insert the appropriate acknowledgment in any subsequent edition.

page 140: Time & Life Pictures/Getty Images;
page 141: Associazione Archivio Storico Olivetti, Ivnea, Italy;
page 142: Courtesy of Archivio Fotografico © La Triennale di Milano;
page 143: Getty Images;
page 144-145: Courtesy of Sir Kenneth Adam, London;
page 146 top left: © 2009. Digital Image, The Museum of Modern Art, New York/ © Photo SCALA, Florence;
page 146 top right: Series 7 chair, designed in 1955 by Arne Jacobsen for Fritz Hansen. www.fritzhansen.com;
page 146 top: Courtesy of TENDO PLY. Fukasawa blg., 2F 4-35-7, Fukasawa, Setagaya-ku, Tokyo, Japan. 158-0081. Tel: 81 3 5758 7111. Fax: 81 3 5758 7112. www.tendo.ne.jp/ply;
page 147 bottom: © Lorenzo Marasso;
page 148 top left: © 2006 Topfoto/Jon Mitchell. Topfoto.co.uk;
page 148 top right: www.lucymooney.com;
page 148 bottom: Photographer: Piero Fasanotto. www.flos.com;
page 149 top: Irina Kalashnikova;
page 149 bottom left: 20th Century Fox/ The Kobal Collection;
page 149 bottom right: courtesy of The Advertising Archives;
page 150: Popperfoto/Getty Images;
page 151 top: Puma City, design by LOT-EK. Puma City, photography: Danny Bright;
page 151 bottom: Photo Mads Mogensen; Styling: Martina Hunglinger. Design: Henning Larsen Architects, Denmark;
page 152 top left: courtesy of The Advertising Archives;
page 152 top right: www.bicworld.com;
page 152 centre: Courtesy of Luxottica Group UK & Ireland;
page 152 bottom: Woodystock/Alamy;
page 153: TfL from the London Transport Museum;
page 154-155: © Slinkachu, from 'Little People in the City', Boxtree;
page 156 top left: Shinypix/Alamy;
page 156 top right: Gaba/G&B Images/Alamy;
page 156 bottom left & right: D. Hurst/Alamy;
page 159: NMeM Daily Herald Archive/Science Museum/SSPL;
page 160: Reproduced by permission of Penguin Books Ltd.;
page 162 top left & top right: courtesy of Tupperware;
page 162 bottom: courtesy of The Advertising Archive;
page 163: NMeM Daily Herald Archive/Science Museum/SSPL;
page 164 top left: www.scp.co.uk;
page 164 top right: ©Swatch Ltd;
page 164 bottom: ©Bodum UK Ltd;

page 165 top: courtesy of Conran & Partners;
page 165 bottom: © Alessi;
page 167: courtesy of the Knoll Archive;
page 168: www.kartell.com;
page 169: Ignazia Favata/Studio Joe Columbo, Milan;
page 170 top: ©Verner Panton Design, Basel, Switzerland;
page 170 centre & bottom: www.vitra.com;
page 171: ©Verner Panton Design, Basel, Switzerland;
page 172-3: ©Verner Panton Design, Basel, Switzerland;
page 174: ©EADS Astrium/C.MEriaux/2007;
page 175 top: Andy Stagg/View Pictures;
page 175 centre: Marc Newson Ltd;
page 175 bottom: ©Ron Arad, One Off Ltd, London, GB. Courtesy of Vitra Design Museum, Weil am Rhein;
page 177: ©Droits reserves/©Collection Centre Pompidou, Dist. RMN/ Jean-Claude Planchet;
page 178: Private Collection/©Wolfgang's Vault/ www.wolfgangsvault.com/The Bridgeman Art Library;
page 179: www.zanotta.it;
page 180: OZ Publications Ink Ltd, from the Collection of Vinmag Archive Ltd;
page 181: Artist: Jamie Reid, courtesy of Isis Gallery, London;
page 182 top left: Braun GmbH;
page 182 top right, bottom right: Jo Klatt/ Braun GmbH;
page 183 top left, top centre: Jo Klatt/ Braun GmbH;
page 183 top right: Braun GmbH;
page 183 centre left, centre centre and centre right: Jo Klatt/Braun GmbH;
page 183 bottom left, bottom centre: Braun Sammlung/Braun GmbH;
page 183 bottom right: Timm Rautert/ Braun GmbH;
page 184 left: Christoph Kicherer/ Jasper Morrison;
page 184 centre: Braun GmbH;
page 184 right: Nokia;
page 185: www.muji.com;
page 186-7: Ford Motor Company Ltd;
page 188: Tom Wood/Alamy;
page 189: courtesy of The Advertising Archive;
page 190-191: Carlo Bavagnoli/Time & Life Pictures/Getty Images;
page 192 top left: www.photolibrary.com;
page 192 top right: www.hille.co.uk
page 192 bottom: www.kartell.com;
page 193: www.kartell.com;
page 194 left: www.gense.se;
page 194 right: www.holmegaard.com;
page 195: Andreas Feininger/Time & Life Pictures/Getty Images;
page 197 top: ©CIO;

page 197 bottom left: Reproduced under the terms of the Click-Use Licence
page 197 bottom right: ©2009 Google – Map Data ©2009 Tele Atlas;
page 198: Redferns/Getty Images;
page 199 top: Alex Dellow/Getty Images;
page 199 bottom right: Popperfoto/ Getty Images;
page 199 bottom left: Neal Preston/Corbis;
page 200-201: Author/Copyright: C J Lim/ Studio 8 Architects;
page 202 top right: Digital Vision/ Photolibrary.com;
page 202 top left: Clive Rose/Getty Images;
page 202 bottom right: Stan Honda/AFP/ Getty Images;
page 202 bottom left: F1 Online/ Photolibrary.com;
page 204: VIEW Pictures Ltd / Alamy;
page 205 top: Fernando Bengoechea/ Beateworks/Corbis;
page 205 bottom: Christopher Cormack/Corbis;
page 206-207: Habitat;
page 208-209: Photos courtesy of Wright. www.wright20.com;
page 210: Toni Vilches / Alamy;
page 211 top left: © 2009. Digital image, The Museum of Modern Art, New York/ © Photo SCALA, Florence;
page 211 top right: Courtesy of Alessi, UK. (N.B. No longer in production);
page 211 bottom: © 2007. Yale University ArtGallery/Art Resource, NY. © Photo SCALA, Florence;
page 213: Lou Linwei/Alamy;
page 214: Carin Katt/Marc Newson Ltd;
page 216 top left: Steve Double;
page 216 top right: Courtesy of Established and Sons;
page 216 bottom: Courtesy of Triflow Concepts;
page 217 top left: Ying Yi Chua/Fabpics/ arcaid.co.uk. Architect: Masterplan by Zaha Hadid;
page 217 top right: Richard Bryant/arcaid.co.uk. Architect: Zaha Hadid;
page 217 bottom right: John Edward Linden/ arcaid.co.uk Architect: Zaha Hadid;
page 217 bottom left: Photography by Zaha Hadid Architects;
page 218-219: G Jackson/arcaid.co.uk Architect: Zaha Hadid Architects;
page 221 left: © 2009. Digital image, The Museum of Modern Art, New York/ © Photo SCALA, Florence;
page 221 right: 02 Photography / Alamy;
page 222: Image courtesy of The Advertising Archives;
page 223: Vladimir Rys/Bongarts/Getty Images;
page 225: Michael Steele/Getty Images;

INDEX

Author's acknowledgments

For making the book possible I would like to thank all the members of the Modern Interiors Research Centre at Kingston University, especially Fiona Fisher; Maureen Hourigan; Jane O'Shea and the staff at Quadrille and Simon Willis. I would also like to thank my daughters, Molly, Nancy and Celia, for their continual support.